3D Fun Facts – I Do, I Did, I'm Done

Celebrity Marriages That Soared, Stumbled, and Spectacularly Imploded

NICCI BROCHARD
&
DR. BEN CHUBA

3D Fun Facts – I Do, I Did, I'm Done

Celebrity Marriages That Soared, Stumbled, and Spectacularly Imploded

CROSSBORDER

New York, London, Quebec

Contents

Introduction

Welcome to the ultimate matrimonial hall of fame and shame, where love stories unfold like reality TV scripts written by caffeinated screenwriters with commitment issues. Celebrity marriages have always fascinated us mere mortals, perhaps because watching the rich and famous navigate the treacherous waters of wedlock makes our own relationship disasters seem charmingly quaint by comparison.

From Hollywood's golden age power couples who built empires together to modern-day social media influencers whose unions last shorter than their viral TikTok videos, the world of celebrity matrimony offers a masterclass in human nature's most bewildering contradictions. These are the people who can memorize Shakespeare soliloquies but apparently never learned the basic principle that signing a prenup while drunk in Vegas might not constitute sound legal planning.

Consider the spectacular irony: individuals who spend millions perfecting their public image somehow repeatedly choose partners with the emotional maturity of houseplants, then act shocked when their fairy-tale romance transforms into a cautionary tale complete with restraining orders and tell-all memoirs. The same celebrities who hire teams of experts to manage their careers, finances, and even their social media posts somehow believe they can win the most complex human relationship without professional guidance.

This collection examines the full spectrum of celebrity matrimonial adventures—the triumphant partnerships that weathered decades of public scrutiny, the train wrecks that provided tabloid editors with early retirement funds, and everything in between. We'll explore unions that began with genuine affection and devolved into bitter custody battles conducted entirely through Instagram stories, alongside marriages that started as publicity stunts but somehow evolved into authentic partnerships.

Each relationship offers valuable insights into the universal challenges of marriage, amplified by the unique pressures of fame, fortune, and having your worst moments dissected by entertainment journalists with the subtlety of hungry vultures. These stories serve as both entertainment and education, revealing how even the most privileged individuals struggle with fundamental human needs for connection, respect, and understanding.

Through expert analysis and behind-the-scenes revelations, we'll uncover the patterns that separate lasting celebrity marriages from spectacular implosions, examining what happens when extraordinary circumstances collide with ordinary human emotions. Buckle up for a journey through love's greatest hits and most notorious flops, where the stakes are measured in both hearts and headlines.

Chapter 1

Cleopatra's Charms:
Nile Politics & Roman Romance

Wrapped in Seduction: Cleopatra's dramatic rug delivery to Julius Caesar

Picture this: It's 48 BC and Cleopatra—former queen-on-the-run, bold as ever—decides to crash Julius Caesar's private quarters in the most extra way imaginable. The young Cleopatra (around 21 and already a seasoned drama queen) had been ousted from power by her kid brother-husband Ptolemy XIII (ancient Egypt was weird like that). But Cleopatra wasn't about to swipe left on opportunity. Knowing she couldn't stroll past her enemies into Alexandria, she had herself smuggled into Caesar's palace rolled up inside a carpet (some say it was a laundry sack, but carpet sounds much cozier). One moment Caesar was settling in for the evening; the next, his guards unroll a rug and out tumbles *the* Cleopatra at his feet. Talk about special delivery – Amazon Prime, eat your heart out.

Cleopatra knew how to make an entrance; one moment Caesar was handling Pharaoh-family drama, the next a gorgeous queen pops out of a rug at his feet (ancient history's most dramatic unboxing). This wasn't just theatrics for theatrics' sake – Cleopatra was making a power move. By personally appearing before Caesar, she bypassed all the murderous palace intrigue and presented herself as *the prize* worth backing. And it worked. The hardened Roman general was reportedly captivated on the spot, charmed by Cleopatra's wit and boldness. After all, how many world leaders get hand-delivered a beauty wrapped in a rug? Caesar, about 30 years her senior and in the midst of a midlife conquest tour, was impressed by the young queen's audacity. Ancient gossip (courtesy of historians like Plutarch and Suetonius) suggests that Caesar was *smitten*. He wined and dined with Cleopatra till dawn on more than one occasion, even fantasizing about a leisurely cruise down the Nile with her if his troops would allow it. In modern terms, Caesar was ready to risk it all – work, reputation, *Rome itself* – for this fascinating femme fatale who literally popped into his life.

Cleopatra wasted no time leveraging her newfound Roman ally-slash-lover. She and Caesar struck a deal: with Caesar's military muscle, Cleopatra would regain her throne, and in return Rome would get a friendly (and fabulously rich) Egypt. It was a political alliance sealed with seduction. Almost overnight, Cleopatra went from exiled queen to Caesar's VIP guest. Her brother Ptolemy XIII? Let's just say things didn't end well for that teen tyrant once Caesar's legions intervened on Cleo's behalf. By the end of the Alexandrian War, Ptolemy was dead (drowned in the Nile, karma's a wet wrap) and Cleopatra was back on top—this time co-ruling with her even younger brother (whom she'd later quietly sideline, as one does). Cleopatra also became a mother: she gave birth to Caesarion, Caesar's son, cheekily nicknamed "Little Caesar" (extra pepperoni, please). It was the ultimate power baby of the ancient world, uniting Rome and Egypt in a bundle of joy and political symbolism.

Ever the diva, Cleopatra even visited Rome with Caesar, causing an absolute sensation. Imagine the buzz in the Roman Forum: *"Have you seen Caesar's Egyptian queen? The one who rides in a golden chariot and wears emeralds the size of your head?"* The Romans were agog at her exotic style—she probably started a few makeup trends two millennia before Hollywood did. Caesar, infatuated, allegedly installed a golden statue of Cleopatra as Isis in a Roman temple, effectively declaring his queen was a living goddess. Bold move, Jules. Rome's elite murmured and tut-tutted (Caesar *was* already married to a proper Roman wife, after all), but the couple didn't care. They were too busy throwing lavish banquets and making history. Of course, every whirlwind romance has its dark clouds. For Cleopatra and Caesar, it came on the Ides of March. When Caesar was assassinated in 44 BC (stabbed 23 times – talk about overkill), Cleopatra's Roman holiday came to an abrupt end. With her protector gone, she packed up her charms (and Caesarion) and hightailed it back to Egypt. Cleopatra was now a widow-mistress in mourning, with a kingdom to run and an uncertain future. Little did she know, the sequel to her love life was waiting in the wings, and it would make the carpet caper with Caesar look tame by comparison.

Empire of Emotion: The fiery love affair and political alliance with Mark Antony

Fast forward a few years: Julius Caesar is dead, Rome is in chaos (again), and Cleopatra is holding things down in Egypt like the boss she is. Enter Mark Antony, one of Caesar's top generals and a notorious party-boy with a heroic resume. Antony had teamed up with Caesar's heir Octavian to hunt down the assassins, but once the revenge tour was done, *surprise!* the victors started squabbling over

Rome. By 41 BC, the Roman world was basically split between Octavian in the west and Mark Antony in the east. Antony, stationed in the east and ever short on cash for his military ambitions, began eyeing Egypt's legendary wealth. Cleopatra, savvy as ever, saw an opportunity. She'd once met Antony in Rome (legend has it she playfully befriended him back then, knowing connections might come in handy). Now Antony summoned Cleopatra to explain her loyalty and, oh by the way, *could she maybe finance his campaign against Parthia?* Cleopatra's response? A grand entrance that left Antony (and everyone else) absolutely gob smacked.

Cleopatra didn't do subtle. When she sailed to meet Antony in the city of Tarsus, she staged the encounter like a Hollywood blockbuster. Actually, scratch that—Hollywood *wishes* it could dream this up. The Egyptian queen arrived on a magnificent river barge with a gilded stern, purple sails billowing in the wind, and silver oars rowing in perfect rhythm to the sound of flutes. Cleopatra herself lounged under a canopy dressed as the goddess Aphrodite (Venus), casually embodying a deity of love and beauty, because why not? To top it off, Cupid-like servants fanned her with feathers while the air wafted with perfume. The people of Tarsus lined the docks with their jaws on the floor, and Mark Antony—this rough, soldier's soldier— was instantly spellbound. It was love at first spectacle. As Plutarch later put it, Cleopatra's allure was "bewitching," and just hearing her voice was a pleasure. Antony, who fancied himself a bit of a new Dionysus (god of wine), had finally met his match in theatrical excess. Cleopatra basically said, "You think you know how to party? Hold my beer (or rather, my wine goblet)" and Antony was *all in*.

From that moment, Antony and Cleopatra became the ancient world's hottest power couple. The chemistry was electric—and so were the political gains. That winter of 41 BC, Antony ditched his military duties (and, ahem, his Roman wife Fulvia) to spend months in Alexandria living the high life with Cleopatra. Imagine the gossip back in Rome: *"Antony's gone native!"* Indeed, he was enjoying the full Cleopatra experience: extravagant feasts every night, hunting and fishing by day, and city-wide pub crawls incognito for kicks. The pair even founded an exclusive drinking club called "The Inimitable Livers," essentially a nightly contest to see whose liver would cry uncle first. They were inseparable lovers *and* co-conspirators, a union of passion and politics. Cleopatra secured Antony's agreement to eliminate her last rivals (bye-bye, pesky sister Arsinoe, exiled no more thanks to an Antony-ordered execution), and in return she pledged Egypt's riches and naval support for Antony's grand plans. The queen had snared another Roman big-shot, but this was no fling—this was an entire empire of emotion.

Cleopatra and Antony's relationship was not just red-hot romantically; it was a full-blown alliance that shook the world. Together they envisioned an eastern empire of their own. And they certainly acted like royalty on a mission. In 37 BC, when Antony temporarily returned to Roman duties, he married Octavian's sister Octavia (political marriages, ugh) to keep the peace. But he couldn't get Cleopatra out of his head (or heart). Before long, he boomeranged back to Alexandria, where Cleopatra greeted him like a queen who knew she had won. They had three children together – including twins named Alexander Helios (Sun) and Cleopatra Selene (Moon). Subtle, right? Antony even declared Cleopatra and Caesarion (her son by

Julius Caesar) as co-rulers of various territories, and showered Cleopatra with titles and lands in an event known as the *Donations of Alexandria*. Essentially, he was handing out chunks of the eastern Mediterranean to his lady and their kids as if writing a will while very much alive. Love makes people do wild things; in Antony's case, it made him play Santa Claus with Roman territories. This did not go over well back in Rome. To Roman conservatives, it looked like Antony had fallen under the spell of a "wicked Oriental sorceress" (cue dramatic eye-roll). In truth, Cleopatra was no sorceress—she was a shrewd stateswoman fluent in nine languages and skilled in politics—but hey, never let facts ruin a good scandal.

Together, Cleopatra and Antony were the it-couple of the East, throwing lavish banquets that made Vegas look like a church picnic. One famous anecdote has Cleopatra betting Antony that she could throw the most expensive dinner party ever. As the story goes, Cleo dissolved one of her priceless pearl earrings in vinegar and drank it, just to win the bet. (If that isn't a flex, I don't know what is. Imagine gulping down a fortune for the sake of *one-upmanship*—Jeff Bezos, take notes.) The two lovers styled themselves as gods on earth; coinage showed them as a divine pair, and they formed their own mini-court of yes-men and revelers. It was glorious, indulgent, and for a brief moment, they ruled like king and queen of a new golden age. But as the saying goes, the higher you climb, the harder you fall. And their fall would be epically hard, courtesy of a Roman rival who was done tolerating this Nile-side fairy tale.

Royal Love Triangle: Rome, Egypt, and betrayal

Every juicy romance needs a villain, and in this saga that role fell to Octavian – Julius Caesar's heir and Mark Antony's co-ruler turned mortal frenemy. From Octavian's perspective, Antony had basically ditched the Roman fam for a foreign queen, and worst of all, he divorced Octavian's sister Octavia in 32 BC. (In the soap opera of Roman politics, that's equivalent to flipping the coffee table at the family dinner.) Thus the stage was set for a royal love triangle of international proportions: Rome's future emperor vs. the star-crossed lovers. Octavian was as straight-laced and calculating as Cleopatra and Antony were flamboyant and passionate. He launched a PR blitz, painting Cleopatra as a sinister seductress who had bewitched poor Antony and was scheming to become Queen of Rome. Romans, eating up the drama, were scandalized: Was Antony even Roman anymore, or had he gone "full Egyptian"? Whispers of betrayal filled the air. Antony sending his Roman wife packing in favor of Cleopatra was the ultimate personal affront to Octavian's family honor, and Octavian milked it for all it was worth. He claimed (with feigned outrage) that Antony was under Cleopatra's thumb, even that Antony planned to give away Rome's eastern provinces to "that woman." The audacity! The betrayal! Clutch your pearls, Roma – this means war.

Octavian cleverly had the Roman Senate declare war on Cleopatra (not on Antony, to make it seem like a righteous crusade rather than a civil spat). It was a genius bit of spin: frame the conflict as Rome versus an exotic queen who ensnared a noble Roman. Never mind that Cleopatra was Antony's partner by choice—Octavian's narrative was that she was a toxic temptress, a "snake" whispering in Antony's ear. Propaganda depicting Cleopatra as a drunken, wanton queen flooded Rome. (Roman tabloids would have had field day if they existed.) Meanwhile in Egypt, Cleopatra and Antony knew a fight was coming and they prepared. In 31 BC their forces faced off against Octavian's navy in the Battle of Actium off the coast of Greece. What ensued was less a glorious showdown and more a disastrous fiasco. Antony and Cleopatra arrayed a huge fleet, but Octavian's top general (Agrippa, a tactical whiz) outmaneuvered them. In the thick of the fight, as Octavian's ships gained the upper hand, Cleopatra made a snap decision: she took her Egyptian ships and fled the battle. Some say she saw the battle was lost; others say it was pre-arranged as an escape plan. Either way, when Queen Cleo's ship hoisted sails and bolted, Antony's heart (and battle plan) shattered. The love-struck general abandoned the fight and chased after Cleopatra with a few ships, leaving the rest of his navy leaderless and confused. (Imagine being one of Antony's soldiers at that moment: "Did our boss just *leave*? Is that allowed?!") Antony's fleet, feeling betrayed and rudderless, soon surrendered to Octavian. The Battle of Actium was an epic fail for the lovers, and a triumph for Octavian. As one ancient account basically put it: *Rome's power couple blew it.* Victorious Octavian, probably doing a smug happy dance, then headed to Egypt to finish the job.

Back in Alexandria, things went from bad to worse. Antony was devastated and angry—mostly at himself, one hopes, but there was tension. Did Cleopatra betray him by fleeing? Did he betray her by not fighting to the death? This was the messiest breakup-that-isn't-really-a-breakup in history. They regrouped for a last stand in Egypt, desperately trying to raise forces, but the odds were grim. Octavian was closing in fast with legions at his back. Cleopatra had a Plan B though (she always had a plan): she prepared her mausoleum and stashed her treasures, determined that if defeat was inevitable, she wouldn't go down without some dramatic flourish. She even tested the waters to negotiate with Octavian, reportedly offering to abdicate or bribe him to spare her children. Octavian, ever the cool customer, kept things cordial but gave no promises—he was playing for time and intended to parade Cleopatra in his triumph back in Rome, a living trophy. Realizing Octavian was not about to let her keep any semblance of power, Cleopatra supposedly considered one last gambit: Could she charm Octavian like she did Caesar and Antony? Unfortunately for her, Octavian was *not* the partying type and had zero interest in a fling with his rival's queen. (He was more into power than romance—think of him as the CEO who won't attend the office party, let alone run off with the office temptress.)

As Octavian's forces entered Alexandria in 30 BC, a tragic comedy of errors unfolded. Accounts vary, but one dramatic tale recounts that Cleopatra, fearing for her life, faked her own suicide to mislead Octavian (and possibly to test Antony's feelings). Her plan misfired spectacularly. When Antony heard a report that Cleopatra was dead, he was utterly undone. In a fit of grief and Roman honor, Antony decided to fall on his sword – literally. He impaled himself, the standard Roman way of saying "I'm out" when all is lost. But in a dark twist, he didn't die immediately. (So much for the clean dramatic exit.) Mortally wounded but still alive, Antony learned Cleopatra was actually *not* dead. In fact, she was holed up in her mausoleum, very much alive and probably shocked by how far the rumor had gone. In one final poignant scene, the bleeding Antony was hauled to Cleopatra's hideout. According to legend, he died in her arms, with

Cleopatra wailing in sorrow. It's the stuff of Shakespearean tragedy – no, really, Shakespeare later dramatized exactly this, melodrama and all. The betrayals here were plentiful and ironic: Antony felt betrayed by fate (and maybe by Cleopatra's ruse), Cleopatra felt betrayed by Octavian's false promises, and the Roman troops felt betrayed by Antony's choices. Basically, trust was in *short* supply at the end of this love triangle.

Marriage Lesson: When you mix an empire with "till death do us part," watch out for snakes—literally

And so we arrive at the final chapter of this wild tale, wherein matrimony meets monarchy and things get *deadly*. Cleopatra and Mark Antony's alliance had been a marriage of love and ambition – they literally tied the knot (by Egyptian rites) and fancied themselves the co-rulers of the world. But when you mix an empire with "till death do us part," the fallout can be lethal. In their case, it involved actual snakes – literally. After Antony's death, Cleopatra was a queen without a king, a mother fearing for her children, and a prisoner in all but name. Octavian finally cornered her. He tried to convince Cleopatra that surrender wasn't so bad – after all, he implied, she'd just be *paraded through Rome in chains* for his Triumph, nbd. Cleopatra was nobody's fool; she knew a life of humiliation (or a quick execution afterward) awaited if she marched in Octavian's victory parade. This proud daughter of the Pharaohs wasn't about to be a sideshow. So she resolved to follow her lover into the great beyond, on her own terms.

Cleopatra's death is the stuff of legend, and like everything else about her, she made sure it was iconic. The popular version (and why not believe it?) is that she arranged to have a poisonous asp (cobra) smuggled into her quarters in a basket of figs. Then, dressed in her royal finery, Cleopatra pressed the asp to her skin. The venom did its work quickly. When Octavian's men finally burst in, they found the 39-year-old queen dead on her golden bed, with two of her loyal serving women also perished at her side. There was likely a note politely informing Octavian that she was *not* going to grace his parade. Talk about committing to a dramatic exit! She took the whole "till death do us part" vow and made it her grand finale – with a snake as the surprise guest. (It gives a whole new meaning to "toxic relationship.") Octavian was reportedly furious; he'd been robbed of his prize exhibit. But he also couldn't help but respect the audacity. Cleopatra had one-upped him in death, denying Rome the spectacle of Queen Cleopatra in chains.

In the aftermath, Octavian did what victors do: he consolidated power. He would soon be known as Augustus, the first Roman Emperor, and Egypt became just another province in Rome's growing empire. He also took a page from the Ancient World Family Values Handbook: seeing to it that Cleopatra's eldest son Caesarion was eliminated (too many potential Caesars is a bad thing for a new Caesar). Ouch. As for Cleopatra and Antony's other children, Octavian spared them, perhaps out of a glimmer of mercy or political calculation. In a twist worthy of daytime TV, Octavia (Antony's Roman ex-wife and Octavian's sister) took in Cleopatra's kids to raise as her own. Yes, the same Octavia whom Antony dumped for Cleopatra ended up mothering the children of that union. If that isn't grace (or absurd irony), what is? One of those kids, Cleopatra Selene, even grew up to be a queen in her own right (marrying an African king). The legacy of Cleopatra literally lived on, scattered across the Mediterranean.

So, what's the marriage lesson in this whole saga? Perhaps it's this: mixing amour and empire is a risky business. Love can make even the smartest leaders throw caution (and kingdoms) to the wind. Cleopatra and Mark Antony's union rocked two civilizations and nearly created a new one, but it also led to their undoing. They learned the hard way that when passion and power entwine, the result can be explosive. Promises were made "till death do us part," and wow did they deliver on that promise—*with interest.* In their case, "watch out for snakes" wasn't just a saying about treachery; it was the literal cause of death and the metaphorical symbol of all the deceit around them. The tale of Cleopatra's charms is a cautionary romantic epic: it has the glamour of a celebrity gossip column, the intrigue of a political thriller, and the pathos of a tragedy. It reminds us that historical figures, despite the crowns and armies, were people moved by love, lust, and ego. Cleopatra used romance as a political tool and politics as a romantic backdrop, and for a while, it made her more powerful than ever. But in the end, even the Queen of the Nile couldn't have it all. Her story lives on as a timeless lesson that love may conquer all – except maybe aspiring Roman emperors with pet snakes. And yet, you can't help but admire Cleopatra's hustle and flair. She played a high-stakes game of love and war and nearly won. If there were an ancient history Oscars, she'd sweep the categories: Best Entrance (inside a rug), Best Original Drama, and Best Exit (via snakebite, dropping the mic on the Roman Empire). Two millennia later, we're still enthralled by her story – and that, dear reader, is the ultimate charm of Cleopatra.

Chapter 2

Six Wives, One Divorce King:
Henry VIII's Matrimonial Mayhem

The Tudor Tinder Swipes: Henry's rapid and ruthless royal selections

Henry VIII looms large in history not just for his political might, but for his six marriages – a matrimonial record so tumultuous it makes modern celebrity love lives look tame. In fact, the famous rhyme "divorced, beheaded, died, divorced, beheaded, survived" neatly sums up the fates of his wives. Henry was wed to his first wife for nearly 25 years – longer than his next five marriages *combined*. If there were a Tudor-era dating app, the king's profile would read something like: *"Monarch seeking fertile young queen. Must love dancing, jewels, and producing baby boys. Swipe right if your name is not Catherine (I've already got three of those)."* Henry's love life was essentially a royal reality show, complete with abrupt eliminations and plot twists worthy of The Bachelor: Palace Edition. And the *Divorce King* played to win, bending church and state to his amorous whims.

To set the stage, young Henry VIII wasn't always the bloated tyrant of portraits; he started off as a charismatic, handsome prince – a 16th-century *heartthrob*. At 17, he married Catherine of Aragon, a Spanish princess who had previously been wed to Henry's older brother (scandalous in theory, but the Pope granted them a special dispensation). For two decades Catherine was the quintessential loyal queen: dignified, deeply Catholic, and popular with the people. She and Henry had one surviving child, Mary, but tragically no sons, as multiple pregnancies ended in miscarriages or infant deaths. By the 1520s, with Henry edging into midlife and no male heir in sight, the king's wandering eye began to rove. It didn't help that Henry believed a biblical curse hung over his marriage – he cited scripture that warned against a man taking his brother's widow, convincing himself that was why God denied him sons. (Never mind that Catherine insisted her first marriage had been unconsummated; Henry was *sure* the Big Guy upstairs was unhappy with his wife choice.) Royal therapists weren't a thing yet, so Henry found his own solution: trade in the wife and reset the "try for son" odometer with a new model.

Enter Anne Boleyn, Catherine's younger, savvy lady-in-waiting. Anne was witty, outspoken, and – crucially – refused to be just another mistress. She friend-zoned the King of England, of all people, holding out for a wedding ring. For Henry, who was used to getting his way in *everything*, Anne's coy resistance was intoxicating. By 1526, the king was utterly infatuated. Imagine the Tudor court grapevine (a.k.a. equivalent of palace Twitter): whispers that the king was writing love letters and composing love songs for Anne, while poor Catherine was left on read. Henry grew *rapidly* impatient to marry Anne. There was just one big problem: the Pope. Catholic rules being rather unfriendly to divorce, the Pope (under pressure from Catherine's nephew, the powerful Emperor Charles V) outright refused to annul Henry's first marriage. So Henry did what any man in a midlife crisis determined to marry his side-chick would do – he created an entirely new church so he could grant himself a divorce. Seriously. In 1533, Henry dumped the Pope like a bad Tinder match, declared himself the Supreme Head of the Church of England, and "annulled" his marriage to Catherine on his own authority. Talk about extreme measures: one day he's *Defender of the [Catholic] Faith*, the next he's head of a DIY Protestant Reformation, all because Rome wouldn't let him swipe right on wife number two.

Catherine of Aragon was unceremoniously banished from court in 1533, cast aside as the newly minted Dowager Princess (Henry retroactively decided her only true husband had been his late brother). After 24 years of marriage, she was essentially divorced and demoted in favor of Anne. The whole ordeal shocked Europe – picture international headlines (or the quill-and-parchment equivalent) screaming "King Dumps Wife, Quits Catholic Church: England in Uproar!" It was the 16th-century version of a celebrity scandal, with Catherine as the sympathetic ex-wife getting cheers from the public. Henry, however, was beyond caring. He had Tudor dynasty business to handle (read: make babies), and Anne Boleyn was the woman he believed would give him the coveted son. As he saw it, he'd sacrificed an entire alliance with Spain and blown up his relationship with the Pope to marry Anne – the stakes were sky-high. With his religious *Tudor Tinder* now fully in his control, the King wasted no time: he married Anne in a secret ceremony (while still awaiting the official annulment) and then publicly in 1533, effectively bigamy with a crown on. Henry's swift wife-swap had all of Europe clutching their rosary beads. But for Henry, this was just another bold move in his ruthless royal selection process. After all, what's a little constitutional crisis when true love (or at least hot lust and an ambition for sons) is on the line?

By the end of this "Tudor Tinder" saga, Henry had perfected the art of rapid spouse rotation. He'd swiped left (in the form of divorce or worse) on queens who displeased him, and he wasn't shy about doing it again. Spoiler alert: Anne Boleyn's tenure would prove brief and *very* dramatic – but more on that in a moment. The pattern was set. Henry VIII treated marriage as a means to an end, and woe to the wife who didn't deliver. A king that creates his own church just to remarry is clearly *not* playing by anyone else's rules. In Henry's court, the marital stakes were literally life and death, and each new queen knew the previous one's fate. As we turn to Anne Boleyn's saga, buckle up: the ride's about to get even bumpier, like a season finale where the star contestant loses more than just the competition – she loses her head.

Anne Boleyn's Fall from Grace: Love, lust, and losing your head

If Anne Boleyn were alive today, she'd break the internet. Her rise was the ultimate Cinderella story – and her fall, the ultimate tragic thriller. Henry's seven-year pursuit of Anne was the stuff of legend: he penned her passionate love letters, lavished her family with titles, and literally restructured England's religion to win her hand. Anne went from lady-in-waiting to Queen of England, crowned in 1533 amid extravagant pageantry, hailed as the kingdom's new hope for male heirs. For a brief, glittering moment, Anne was "the most happy" (as she proclaimed in her royal motto) and Henry was besotted. But oh, how quickly the Tudor tables turn. By 1536, less than three years into the marriage, Queen Anne would learn that *falling in love* with Henry VIII was far easier than staying alive as his wife.

In the beginning, Anne played her cards brilliantly. She refused to sleep with Henry until they were wed, leveraging his infatuation to ascend from mere noblewoman to queen. It worked – perhaps *too* well. The couple's early days were like a honeymoon montage: Henry showering Anne with gifts and honors (he even made her *Marquess of Pembroke* in her own right), and Anne basking in the attention. But the good times came with enormous pressure. In September 1533, Anne gave birth to her first child – a healthy girl named Elizabeth, the future Elizabeth I. Henry publicly feigned joy, but privately you can imagine him thinking, "Cute kid, but where's my boy?" The clock was ticking for Anne to produce a son. Over the next two years, she suffered miscarriages, including the loss of a male infant. Each disappointment frayed Henry's devotion. The King who once wrote love poems for Anne began flirting with her ladies-in-waiting (ever the pattern with him). Anne, fiery and proud, didn't tolerate Henry's affairs quietly as Catherine had. Reports say she unleashed her temper and jealousy, which only irked Henry more. The royal marriage, built on passion, started cracking under stillborn hopes and mutual mistrust.

By early 1536, Henry's wandering eye had fixed on a new lady-in-waiting: Jane Seymour, a demure contrast to the outspoken Anne. Sensing an opportunity, Henry's advisors – led by the wily Thomas Cromwell – moved to solve the "Anne problem." What unfolded next feels ripped from a *Game of Thrones* episode or a particularly dark reality TV twist. Suddenly, Anne Boleyn was accused of adultery, incest, and treason, charges so lurid and shocking that everyone at court's jaws hit the floor. The notion that the queen had betrayed Henry with multiple lovers (including her own brother!) was scandalous – and historians widely believe the charges were trumped-up nonsense. But in the spring of 1536, truth mattered little. Henry *needed* Anne gone, and conveniently these accusations would rid him of her *and* any pesky need for another divorce. The queen was arrested and thrown in the Tower of London. A jury of noblemen – including, cruelly, her former fiancé Henry Percy – found her guilty. Anne was condemned to death for high treason against her lord and husband.

The fall from grace was lightning-fast. One day Anne was the glamorous queen; the next, she was an outcast in a cold tower cell, waiting for the axe. To her credit, Anne maintained her innocence with dignity. She reportedly quipped that she had "*the mouth of a sinner, but the heart of a saint,*" denying the outrageous charges. On May 19, 1536, Anne Boleyn climbed the scaffold at the Tower Green. In a final, poignant speech, she praised Henry (perhaps hoping to protect their young daughter Elizabeth's position) and refrained from hurling any curses – a classy exit for a queen about to meet a cruel fate. In an act of grim mercy (or morbid showmanship), Henry had dispatched an expert French swordsman to perform the execution, rather than the usual clumsy axe. With a single swift stroke, Anne Boleyn was beheaded, literally losing her head as poetic justice for "losing her head" in love and ambition.

Thus ended the reign of Wife #2 – a meteoric rise and a horrific fall, all because she couldn't give Henry a son and *dared* to challenge the King's ego. It's hard to overstate the courtroom-turned-circus atmosphere of Anne's downfall. Imagine a modern tabloid cover: "*Queen Anne on Trial: Infidelity and Incest Shocker!*" The Tudor court was ablaze with gossip. Common folks couldn't believe the same woman for whom Henry split from the Church was now executed as a cheater. Anne's death sent a chilling message: in Henry's world, queens were disposable. As one contemporary cynic quipped, "*Old Testament Henry – if she doth vex thee, cut her off.*" The king, apparently unbothered by executing the woman he'd once moved heaven and earth to marry, didn't even pause for mourning. In a plot twist that would be deemed too far-fetched in fiction, Henry betrothed Jane Seymour the very next day and married her just 11 days after Anne's execution. Yes, the man moved on faster than a Netflix autoplay. Talk about a rebound relationship – Henry practically had Jane waiting in the wings while Anne was hauled off to the scaffold.

Anne Boleyn's dramatic arc — from love and lust to a headless ghost — solidified Henry's notorious reputation. He had now divorced one wife and beheaded another. Europe was aghast; the French king allegedly joked that his own wives were lucky to be safe in France away from England's wife-killer king. For modern observers, Anne's story reads like a royal cautionary tale: *beware a king who breaks rules for you, because he can break you too.* Yet for Henry, this was merely the midway point of his matrimonial mayhem. The soap opera continued, and next up was the seemingly perfect Jane Seymour, who would finally give England what it desperately wanted: a male heir. Would that satisfy our divorce-happy monarch? Spoiler: Henry's heart is a bottomless pit – or perhaps more accurately, a conveyor belt for queens. On to the next episode!

Jane Seymour: The Favorite (Until She Died)

In the revolving door of Henry VIII's wives, Jane Seymour managed to do what her predecessors could not – give the king a son. That singular achievement earned Jane a glowing reputation in Henry's memory, and historians often dub her the king's "favorite" wife. But let's not get ahead of ourselves: Jane's story, though mercifully short on scandal, is still steeped in the palace intrigue that characterized Henry's court. She was Wife #3, the immediate replacement for Anne Boleyn, and the contrast between the two women could not have been sharper. Where Anne was fiery, outspoken, and flirtatious, Jane was demure, gentle, and utterly devoted to obeying the King. Frankly, that's probably a big part of why she survived the court's cutthroat politics (at least until childbirth did her in). Jane basically rolled out the Tudor welcome mat and said, *"Your Majesty, I'll be the angelic wife you've been waiting for,"* and Henry – reeling from Anne's tumultuous end – was all too happy to believe her.

The circumstances of Jane Seymour's rise were eyebrow-raising to say the least. Henry was betrothed to Jane the day after Anne Boleyn's execution, and they formally married within eleven days. The ink on Anne's death warrant was barely dry when Jane stepped into the spotlight in a wedding dress. You have to picture it: Tudor wedding bells ringing while Anne's French swordsman was probably still packing to sail home. If Twitter existed, #TooSoon would have been trending. But in Henry's mind, why wait? He'd finally rid himself of the "treacherous" Anne and now had a meek, blonde Tudor rose who promised him domestic peace – and sons. Jane, for her part, had seen two queens fall (she'd served Catherine of Aragon and Anne Boleyn as a lady-in-waiting) and she learned *exactly* what not to do. Her motto as queen was literally "Bound to obey and serve," a not-so-subtle pledge to Henry that she'd be the anti-Anne. She avoided the flashy French fashions Anne loved, opting for traditional English modesty. She even reportedly mended Henry's relationship with his first daughter, Mary, which was a savvy move – playing peacemaker endeared her to the king. But Jane was no fool; when she gently suggested Henry restore Mary to the succession, Henry sharply reminded her of Anne's fate with a cold, *"Remember what happened to the last queen when she meddled"*. Gulp. Jane took the hint and stuck to nursery planning.

Fortunately for Jane, her tenure as queen was free of the drama that haunted Catherine and Anne – at least on the surface. There were no public showdowns, no juicy love triangle gossip. Henry *truly seemed content* with Jane. Contemporary accounts describe him doting on his quiet wife. The reason was simple: by late 1537, Jane Seymour had done the one thing Henry valued above all – she bore him a male heir. On October 12, 1537, after a long and difficult labor, Queen Jane delivered Prince Edward. The court rejoiced; cannons fired in celebration, and grown men wept with relief. Henry was 46 and had been waiting decades for this moment. He declared the day one of the happiest of his life. Finally, a legitimate son to secure the Tudor dynasty! Henry's joy and public adoration of Jane skyrocketed. He called her his "true and loving wife," and people whispered that Jane had succeeded in taming the beast. In portraits, Jane is depicted with a serene smile, as if she knew she'd hit the jackpot: she gave the king what he wanted, and in return he gave her his heart (insofar as Henry had one left to give).

But in a tragic twist worthy of Shakespeare, Jane Seymour's story ended just as her triumph began. Not long after Prince Edward's birth, Jane fell gravely ill – likely due to childbed fever, a common postpartum infection in those days. Henry was frantic. This was the wife he actually *loved* (or at least never got around to disliking), and she was slipping away due to natural causes – a fate outside his control for once. Despite prayers and medical quackery (the royal physicians tried everything short of sacrificing a goat), Jane died on October 24, 1537, less than two weeks after giving birth. Henry was genuinely heartbroken. The man who had barely blinked at discarding wives now went into deep mourning. He donned black, shut himself away, and reportedly cried for his lost Jane. In a move that speaks volumes, Henry later chose to be buried beside Jane at St. George's Chapel in Windsor – a posthumous honor he didn't give to any other wife. It was as if Henry acknowledged that Jane was the one who fulfilled his ultimate wish and earned a permanent spot in his infamy... er, heart.

Jane's death elevated her to near-sainthood in Henry's eyes. He told anyone who'd listen that Jane was "his only true wife," conveniently forgetting how infatuated he'd been with wives one and two. (Selective memory is strong with this king.) Of course, cynics at court noted that Jane's saintly image benefited from timing – she died before Henry ever got bored or angry with her. "The perfect wife," one courtier jibed, "is a dead one," meaning Jane never had the chance to disappoint Henry or face his wrath. Dark humor aside, Jane's short queenship did accomplish something monumental: she stabilized the Tudor succession by producing Edward. Even though Henry had two healthy daughters, in the 16th century a son was the real prize. Jane delivered that prize and thus secured her legacy as the wife who succeeded where others failed.

Henry waited a decent interval after Jane's passing – for him, anyway. For over two years, he remained single, which was practically celibate by his standards. Some say he truly mourned Jane; others note he was busy doting on baby Edward and brutally quelling a rebellion (the Pilgrimage of Grace) that had flared up over his religious changes. By 1539, however, the show had to go on. Henry was aging and shockingly, he contemplated the unromantic notion of marrying for political alliance rather than passion this time. That brings us to wife number four. But before we swipe to the next bride, let's acknowledge Jane's unique status. In the chaotic wife roulette of Henry's life, Jane Seymour was the house favorite – the one who won the jackpot (briefly) and escaped the axe by fate's mercy. The king's favorite wife was also the one he didn't personally have to get rid of. Jane exited on a high note, leaving Henry with the son he'd desperately sought and a rosy memory unsullied by the usual drama. Little Edward's future was bright, Henry's dynastic paranoia was eased, and for a fleeting moment, *all was well in Tudor Land.* Of course, with Henry's track record, stability never lasts long. The *Divorce King* was about to return to form, proving that even after finding "the one," he just couldn't resist spinning the marital wheel a few more times.

Marriage Lesson: Beware the man who creates his own church just to remarry

By the time Henry VIII took his fourth wife, one would think any eligible lady in Europe would know the gigantic red flags waving over this king. Here was a man who literally changed his country's religion to ditch one wife and behead another – the sixteenth-century equivalent of "it's not me, it's you (and God said so)." If Henry were on a modern dating app, his bio might include a disclaimer: *"Warning: will break with Rome for love. Also, might execute if unhappy."* It sounds absurd, but that's essentially the marriage lesson Henry's life offers: beware the guy who will upend an entire church for his marital convenience. It's the ultimate red flag, and in Henry's case, later wives tread with caution (not that it always saved them).

After Jane Seymour's death, Henry's advisors convinced him to marry quickly again – England still needed backup heirs and international allies. So in 1540, in came Anne of Cleves, a German princess. Their union was arranged from afar, with Henry relying on a painted portrait for her looks (think of it as the original online dating profile picture). Famously, when Anne arrived in person, Henry took one look and declared, "I like her not!" The poor woman wasn't to the king's taste physically – history gossip claims Henry complained of her appearance (the legend is he called her a "Flanders mare," though that quote may be apocryphal). In modern terms, Henry felt catfished by the portrait. The marriage went unconsummated and embarrassingly brief. But here's one wife-swap with a surprisingly happy ending: rather than meeting the usual cruel fate, Anne of Cleves agreed to an annulment within six months. She smartly took a deal to become the King's "Beloved Sister," receiving a generous settlement – palaces, money, and freedom. Anne of Cleves even stayed friends with Henry (she outlived him and all the other wives, earning the unofficial title of "Luckiest Ex" in Tudor history). The lesson from Wife #4: sometimes divorcing Henry VIII *peacefully* was possible, but it required zero romantic entanglement and a willingness to walk away *fast* with a nice severance package.

Henry's fifth wife, however, wasn't so fortunate. Catherine Howard was a teenage cousin of Anne Boleyn, tossed into Henry's path by scheming relatives eager to regain favor. Catherine was *approximately 19* to Henry's nearly 50, an absurd age gap even by Tudor standards. Initially, the aging king was besotted by Catherine's youth and beauty – she was playful and vivacious, bringing a bit of sunshine to the grumpy, overweight monarch. In 1540 they married, and Henry swooned like an old fool in love, calling her his "rose without a thorn." But this May-December marriage had disaster written all over it. The naïve teen queen found life as wife to a obese, ailing king (with a festering leg wound and a short temper) less glamorous than anticipated. Catherine made the *fatal error* of seeking affection elsewhere. Before long, gossip of her adultery with a handsome courtier, Thomas Culpeper, reached Archbishop Cranmer. Worse, it emerged Catherine had a rather *scandalous past* (she'd had a sexual relationship with a gentleman named Francis Dereham before marriage). Once again, Henry's pride was pierced – his pretty young wife had played him for a fool. The *royal wrath* was swift and terrible. In 1542, barely a year and a half into the marriage, Catherine Howard was executed for treason, the same charge that doomed her cousin Anne. The young queen supposedly screamed for mercy all the way to the chopping block, but mercy was one thing Henry had long run out of. So Catherine Howard became the second of Henry's wives to meet the headsman, reinforcing the marriage lesson: a husband who's beheaded one wife for cheating isn't likely to tolerate a cheating second. (*Memo to future trophy spouses: maybe don't conduct your affair in your husband's palace.*)

Finally, we come to Catherine Parr, wife number six – a woman astute enough to survive where others perished. By 1543, Henry was a hulking, irascible 52-year-old in failing health. Catherine Parr, twice-widowed and in her thirties, was practically a senior citizen by Tudor bridal standards (she was also *named Catherine*, because apparently Henry had a thing for that name). She didn't particularly want to marry the king – rumor has it she was in love with Sir Thomas Seymour – but when the King of England says "Marry me," you don't say "No, thanks." Thus Catherine Parr became the final queen consort to Henry. She was more of a nurse and companion than a romantic partner. To her credit, Catherine Parr was highly educated and even authored a book – a rare accomplishment for a woman then. She skillfully navigated Henry's mood swings and even reconciled him with his two daughters, Mary and Elizabeth, helping restore them to the line of succession. However, even this savvy survivor had a close brush with disaster: Catherine held strong Protestant sympathies and once engaged Henry in a theological debate that *almost* landed her an arrest warrant for heresy. When she realized her mistake, Catherine quickly apologized and mollified the king, essentially sweet-talking her way out of execution. "I was merely disputing to take your mind off your pain, dear husband," she cooed, and Henry, miraculously, bought it. The warrant was torn up, and Catherine Parr lived to see another day. She would be the only wife to outlive Henry, who died in 1547 with Catherine by his side (probably relieved as anyone that this dangerous game was finally over). Catherine Parr's reward for surviving Henry? Freedom to marry her true love (Thomas Seymour) a few months later – though in a final ironic twist, that romance ended poorly too. But at least she kept her head under Henry, which is more than some could say.

Looking back on Henry VIII's matrimonial mayhem, the modern parallels are striking and darkly comic. This was a king treating wives like seasonal fashion – discard the old, bring in the new – with *fatal* consequences for some. It's as if Henry saw himself as the star of a never-ending reality show: *The Real Housewives of Tudor England,* where he was executive producer and elimination was literal. His court was as vicious as any tabloid-filled Hollywood scene, and Henry was the ultimate diva, ready to axe (literally) those who fell out of favor. The man created a whole new Church of England to legitimize swapping out Wife #1 for Wife #2. Anne Boleyn quipped in the modern musical Six that "I broke England from the church – I'm that sexy", and indeed Henry's desire for Anne changed the course of English history. Talk about being *extra*: many men bring flowers or write poems; Henry brought down a centuries-old religious establishment to get remarried. When that marriage soured, he proved he was just as willing to break *heads* as he was to break with Rome.

So, what's the take-home lesson from the Divorce King's saga? Power and passion are a volatile mix – and if your suitor has a track record of beheading exes, maybe swipe left. Henry VIII's life reads like a royal cautionary tale to *beware the red flags*: he was charismatic, wealthy, and powerful, yes, but also egotistical, impulsive, and increasingly tyrannical. His six wives learned, in various tragic ways, that being married to a man who sees himself as God's anointed (and acts accordingly) is a perilous gig. In the end, Henry got his long-sought male heir, but in a twist of fate, that son (Edward VI) died as a teen. Instead, it was Henry's daughters – Mary and Elizabeth – who would reign after him, the very outcomes he twisted himself in knots to avoid. The joke was on Henry: the "spares" he sidelined became the heirs who shaped England's future. Elizabeth I, Anne Boleyn's daughter, would go on to be one of England's greatest monarchs, a poignant postscript to Anne's ill-fated love affair.

Henry VIII's matrimonial mayhem left a lasting legacy in culture and law (he's the reason *divorce* and *church* got so entangled in England), but it also left us with one heck of a story – a real-life soap opera that still captivates. It's got everything: romance, betrayal, political upheaval, religious schism, and a body count. And through it all, one can't help but chuckle at the sheer audacity of this king who serially wed and de-wed as if the rules simply didn't apply (because, in his mind, they didn't). Henry's life is a reminder that truth is stranger than fiction and that absolute power not only corrupts absolutely – it marries recklessly. So next time you see a dramatic celebrity divorce or a wild reality dating show, just remember King Henry VIII, the *OG* Divorce King. Six wives, two beheadings, two divorces, a deceased favorite, and one survivor – it's a tale as juicy and dramatic as any modern scandal, proving that when it comes to outrageous marital drama, Henry set a bar so high (or low) that few have ever since matched. Lesson learned: if he has to create his own church just to marry you, you might want to check the return policy on that wedding.

Chapter 3

Napoleon's Love Empire:
Joséphine to Marie-Louise

From Prison Widow to Empress: Joséphine's unlikely rise.

Joséphine de Beauharnais's rise to royalty is the kind of plot that would make The Crown writers say "nah, too far-fetched." Born Marie-Josèphe-Rose Tascher de La Pagerie in Martinique, she was shipped off to France in an arranged marriage to Alexandre de Beauharnais, a vain aristocrat who ended up losing his head (literally) during the Revolution. Joséphine herself nearly joined him under the guillotine—talk about dating drama—but a last-minute plot twist (the fall of Robespierre) saved her neck. By 1794, at age 32, she was a widow with two kids, no money, and even her teeth in bad shape (years of sugar plantation living had ravaged her smile). In modern terms, she was at rock bottom, the Real Housewife of the Reign of Terror whose husband literally lost *the ultimate divorce case.*

Yet Joséphine was nothing if not resourceful. Think of her as a social influencer avant la lettre: she secured loans, got a chic little apartment in Paris, and set out to *network* her way back into high society. And by "network," we mean she expertly worked the era's elite dating scene. After a series of affairs with powerful figures, she caught the eye of Paul Barras – basically the political kingpin of post-

Revolution France. When Barras got bored of her, he didn't ghost her; he played matchmaker and introduced her to a rising young artillery officer at a ball in 1795. Enter Napoléon Bonaparte, a man with big dreams and, at that stage, a relatively small bank account. Little did Barras know he was handing Joséphine the golden ticket: within a few years that lovestruck artillery officer would crown himself Emperor, and Joséphine would ride shotgun to the throne.

At first, Joséphine wasn't exactly swooning. The stylish widow reportedly called Napoléon a "puss in boots" behind his back and sniffed at his modest Corsican family background as a "family of beggars". (Imagine a society diva today rolling her eyes at a tech geek's lack of pedigree – that was Joséphine with Napoléon.) But Napoléon was determined. He courted her with the fervor of a Netflix rom-com hero, showering her with gifts and even charming her children with playtime. By March 1796, just months after meeting, they were married – scandalizing Napoléon's family, who thought this glamorous older widow with baggage (two kids, oh mon Dieu!) was beneath their precious Nap. Napoléon, however, was utterly besotted. He had to leave for military duty in Italy two days after the wedding, but he made sure Joséphine (whom he had lovingly nicknamed, insisting she use her middle name "Joséphine" instead of Rose) remembered him. From the field, the 26-year-old general sent a barrage of passionate love letters that could make Shakespeare blush. "Every moment separates me further from you, my beloved… You are the constant object of my thoughts," he gushed. In today's world, we'd say he blew up her phone with texts day and night – *zero chill.*

Joséphine's response? Let's just say the vibe was more *"thanks, luv u, ttyl"* than *"I burn for you."* She wrote far fewer letters back, and her tone was, in Napoléon's words, "cold as friendship". Ouch. While Napoléon was out winning battles and penning steamy missives, Joséphine was enjoying Parisian high life – perhaps *too much.* She dallied with a handsome young cavalry officer named Hippolyte Charles on the side. Yes, our Empress-to-be was essentially pulling a Real Housewives move: hubby's away, time to play. By the time she finally traveled to join Napoléon in Italy (bringing her 23-year-old lover in tow, no less), gossip about her infidelity was the talk of Parisian salons. Napoléon started catching on in late 1796. Arriving at Joséphine's residence in Milan to find her out *shopping* (or so he was told), he grew suspicious. He reacted with a letter that can only be described as emoji mashup in prose: first rage, then desperate passion. "I don't love you anymore; on the contrary, I detest you," he ranted, calling her "a vile, mean, beastly slut", only to follow with "Soon, I hope, I will be holding you in my arms... covering you with a million hot kisses, burning like the equator". Talk about mixed signals – it's basically "I hate you, please come home, xoxo." Napoléon's army might've been conquering Italy, but Love was conquering *him.*

By 1798, the cat was out of the bag (or rather, the puss in boots was out of Paris). Napoléon definitively learned of Joséphine's affair and was furieux. The French general, known for crushing enemies, now faced an opponent he couldn't outflank: *heartbreak.* In a melodrama worthy of a telenovela, he even wrote to his brother declaring he was going to divorce Joséphine. That letter got intercepted by the British – who gleefully published it in newspapers to embarrass the man they called "the Corsican ogre." Cue the 18th-century equivalent of a leaked celebrity text scandal; everyone was sipping tea (quite literally in Britain) over Napoléon's marital woes. Joséphine, on her side, wrote breathlessly to Hippolyte, "Only you can restore me to happiness. Tell me that you love me, that you love only me!" Clearly, *The Bonapartes* was the hottest reality show in Europe. Napoléon, not to be outdone, started an affair of his own during his Egyptian campaign with a young Frenchwoman (Pauline Fourès, nicknamed "Napoleon's Cleopatra"). Hell hath no fury like a *Bonaparte* scorned.

Despite all the adultery and drama, the strange thing is that Napoléon and Joséphine just couldn't quit each other. Napoléon returned to Paris in October 1799, fresh from military glory, to find his wife mortified and begging forgiveness for her trespasses. She literally had to camp outside his door in tears (a scene so dramatic it belongs in *Bridgerton*), until his stepchildren – her kids Hortense and Eugène – convinced him to let her in. Napoléon caved. He couldn't resist her apologies and charms, and he certainly loved her children (whom he would later adopt). The divorce was called off, and by the time Napoléon staged his bloodless coup to seize power in November 1799, Joséphine was by his side as First Consul's lady. They had survived their trial by scandal, though not without scars. The trust between them never fully recovered; Napoléon would openly keep mistresses in later years, and Joséphine knew her days of carefree flirtation were over if she wanted to keep her man (and her head).

Even as other women came and went, Napoléon's deep attachment to Joséphine endured. "My mistresses do not in the least engage my feelings... My mistress is power," he famously quipped in 1804. Power was his true passion, but who was right there sharing that power? Joséphine. In December 1804, Napoléon crowned himself Emperor Napoléon I in a lavish ceremony at Notre-Dame, then turned and crowned Joséphine as Empress. Imagine the scene: the upstart Corsican general placing a glittering crown on the head of the elegant Creole widow – *his* queen of hearts – under the gaze of the Pope, his family, and a who's who of Europe. (He actually took the crown from the Pope's hands to do it himself, a boss move to show he owed his throne to no one.) Joséphine, draped in imperial robes, reportedly wept tears of joy. It was the ultimate triumph of their unlikely love story. Just ten years earlier she'd been locked in a dank prison cell awaiting execution; now she was literally wearing a crown in Notre-Dame. Talk about a glow-up. If this were a movie, we'd roll credits here on the happy ending. But real life, especially with Napoléon, is never that simple – there's always another plot twist around the corner.

Annulment by Emperor: When dynasty trumps devotion

The newly minted Emperor and Empress enjoyed a golden few years at the top. Joséphine embraced the role of imperial consort with aplomb – patronizing arts, setting fashion trends, and turning their home at Malmaison into a paradise of gardens (her famous rose garden was the Versailles of roses) and exotic animals. She had the style; Napoléon had the stature (figuratively speaking, of course). Together, they projected the image of a stable, loving monarchy. But there was one glaring void behind the scenes: no baby Bonaparte. Napoléon's extended family – a cadre of ambitious brothers and sisters – were pressuring him about succession almost as soon as he grabbed the throne. By 1807, it was an open issue: *Who would inherit the empire?* Napoléon had crowned himself *Emperor of the French*, but fate had not crowned him *Father*.

It wasn't for lack of trying. Joséphine had conceived once or twice early in the marriage, but sadly suffered miscarriages (or so it's believed). By her mid-40s, it became apparent that childbearing was unlikely. In 1806, one of Napoléon's mistresses, Éléonore Denuelle, conveniently produced a healthy baby boy, proving that Napoléon's ammo was in working order and the issue lay with 43-year-old Joséphine's fertility. As if Napoléon's ego needed more prodding, tragedy struck in 1807: his beloved nephew Napoléon-Charles – the toddler son of Napoléon's brother Louis and Joséphine's daughter Hortense – died of croup at age 4. This child had been tacitly treated as Napoléon's heir, so his death left Napoléon heir-less and alarmed. To Napoléon's dynastic mind, this was a Code Red. He started drawing up a short list of eligible princesses across Europe as potential new wives, as casually as if he were drafting battle plans. Imagine a powerful CEO making a spreadsheet of younger women to replace his accomplished wife simply because he needs a son to take over the "family business" – that's essentially what happened.

For Joséphine, this looming threat was devastating. She knew well that her inability to produce a child was her Achilles' heel. Ever the savvy operator, she tried everything from healing waters to prayers, and she *dreaded* the day Napoléon might choose duty over love. That day came in late 1809. After years of hemming and hawing, Napoléon finally made the painful decision: he would divorce Joséphine in order to remarry and sire an heir. Or, in the polite terms of monarchy, their marriage would be annulled – as if the whole epic love story had been just a bureaucratic error. In December 1809,

Napoléon broke the news to Joséphine. The scene was heartbreakingly dramatic: upon hearing the words, she reportedly collapsed, sobbing uncontrollably on the floor. Even the iron-willed Emperor cried. This was not a case of "It's not you, it's me." This was "It's not you, it's my need for a baby and political stability." Dynasty trumped devotion.

In a move that could rival any conscious-uncoupling PR statement today, Napoléon and Joséphine handled their split with public grace (at least once the smelling salts were put away). On 15 December 1809, a grand but somber divorce ceremony was held in the Tuileries Palace. The imperial couple sat on two thrones, and in front of assembled courtiers they each read prepared statements affirming their mutual affection *even as they parted*. If tabloids had existed, the headline would've been: *"We Will Always Love Each Other, But France Needs an Heir."* Joséphine, dignified through her tears, affirmed that she "shall ever remain grateful for the love of a great man who has been the glory of France." Napoléon then stood and paid tribute to the woman who had been his partner through all his triumphs and trials. "Far from ever finding cause for complaint," he declared, "I can, on the contrary, only congratulate myself on the devotion and tenderness of my beloved wife". Yes, you read that right – in the very act of *dumping her*, he basically said, *she's perfect and it's heartbreaking that I have to do this*. It was an extraordinarily tender goodbye, akin to a king abdicating his personal happiness for the sake of the realm.

With that, the marriage was nullified (legally, they framed it as if the original 1796 ceremony hadn't met some technical requirements, a little convenient loophole to keep the Pope happy). Joséphine left the palace, no longer Empress – but she didn't leave Napoléon's heart. He ensured she kept the title Empress Dowager in all but name. He gave her the splendid Château de Malmaison and a hefty allowance, and they continued to correspond affectionately. (It was the least he could do after 13 years of her putting up with his *and* his family's antics. Napoléon's sisters had never liked Joséphine and were probably popping champagne at this divorce party, but that's another story.) The newly single Napoléon didn't stay single long – emperors rarely do. He went wife-hunting among the royal families of Europe as if casting the next season of *The Bachelor: Imperial Edition*. The criteria? Young, healthy, and preferably with a womb dynastically certified "proven breeder."

Initially, Napoléon slid into the DMs (okay, sent formal proposals) of the Romanov family – he asked Tsar Alexander I for his teenage sister Grand Duchess Anna. When the Russians balked or delayed (they found the idea of their princess marrying a parvenu Corsican a bit icky), Napoléon turned to his former enemies, the Habsburgs of Austria. To the astonishment of every blue-blood in Europe, the Austrian Emperor said "Yes." Frankly, Emperor Francis II of Austria was terrified of Napoléon after being whupped in multiple wars, and marrying off his daughter to the French conqueror seemed a decent peace offering. So, quick as a musket shot, a marriage was arranged between 40-year-old Napoléon and 18-year-old Archduchess Marie-Louise of Austria. If you're keeping score, Marie-Louise was the *niece* of the late Marie Antoinette – talk about historical irony. The Austrian teenage princess had grown up hearing bedtime stories of how the French Revolution killed her great-aunt Antoinette, and now she was shipping off to France to marry the man who had *dethroned her own father as Holy Roman Emperor*. For

Napoléon, it was the ultimate power move: ditch your true love to marry the daughter of your old nemesis. It's as if a CEO divorced his beloved wife and then married the daughter of a rival CEO to secure a merger. Scandalous? Yes. Effective? We'll see…

Marie-Louise: The Political Rebound

Napoléon's marriage to Marie-Louise in 1810 was the 19th-century equivalent of a midlife crisis rebound. Instead of a sports car, Napoléon acquired a teenaged Habsburg bride. Think of it as "trophy wife diplomacy." On paper, the match checked all the boxes: Marie-Louise brought the prestige of the ancient royal house of Austria and, crucially, a youthful ability to bear children. But let's be real – this was less *romance* and more Game of Thrones. Napoléon himself admitted that he was marrying a womb (not very romantic, Boney!). The French people, ever pragmatic, accepted the swap; many actually hoped a fertile young Empress would secure the imperial succession. Joséphine was loved, but France wanted a baby Bonaparte in the cradle. As one Parisian wit quipped at the time, "No heir, no Empire."

Marie-Louise, for her part, approached the marriage with the enthusiasm of a girl told to eat her vegetables. She had zero say in the matter. Initially she was terrified – imagine being a teenager shipped off to marry the big bad wolf of Europe, who also happens to be twice your age and famously temperamental. (She'd seen the propaganda – Napoléon was depicted in Austrian tales as a sort of Corsican boogeyman.) But duty called, and to her credit, Marie-Louise resolved to do it *properly*. Upon meeting Napoléon, she reportedly found him more charming than expected. Napoléon, ever eager, couldn't even wait for the official ceremony; he rode out to meet her carriage halfway and surprised her by leaping in to give her a first kiss –

scandalously skipping some ceremonial steps. This guy was nothing if not impatient, both on the battlefield and in the bedroom. They were married by proxy in March 1810 and then had a grand Paris wedding in April with all the pomp and cake you'd expect. Think royal wedding fever, Empire edition: huge crowds, fireworks, and probably some snarky pamphlets comparing the new girl to Joséphine (exes loom large, after all).

To Napoléon's relief and delight, the political rebound worked like a charm – biologically at least. Barely one year into the marriage, in March 1811, Marie-Louise delivered a healthy baby boy, Napoléon "*II*", pompously titled the King of Rome. The news was met with celebrations so loud across France, it was like the World Cup and New Year's Eve combined. At last, an heir! Napoléon was over the moon, handing out bonuses to soldiers and christening monuments in the boy's honor. He might have even thought, for a fleeting moment, that he'd outsmarted destiny: he had secured his dynasty and maintained his empire. In those early days, Napoléon was quite affectionate with Marie-Louise. Contemporary letters and accounts suggest he behaved like a gentleman and a proud husband. Marie-Louise wrote to her family that Napoléon was kind to her, and she seemed content enough being adored and showered with jewels. She was no fiery Joséphine, but she was a compliant, sweet young wife who never challenged him – exactly what a control enthusiast like Napoléon ordered from the universe. In modern relationship terms, after years of a passionate, tumultuous marriage (with a partner who would sass him back), Napoléon opted for a *drama-free partnership*. It was more tranquil, but also, let's face it, a bit boring. There were no legendary love letters this time – Napoléon wasn't staying up late writing poetry to Marie-

Louise. Instead, he'd inquire about her health and thank her for giving him a son. It was cordial, dutiful, and devoid of the wild sparks that characterized his life with Joséphine.

Of course, there's a plot twist: it didn't last. Not the marriage per se (that limped on), but the *Empire*. Napoléon's brilliant star soon careened toward disaster. Perhaps feeling invincible after all these domestic accomplishments, Napoléon made the classic blunder of invading Russia in 1812 – the military equivalent of "I bet I can eat just one more slice of pizza" and then regretting it. The campaign was a catastrophic failure, and by 1813 a coalition of angry nations (including dear Papa-in-law Austria) was closing in on France. Marie-Louise was made Regent while Napoléon was off at war – nominally she was in charge in Paris, but in reality she was a 21-year-old with no experience, guided (or manipulated) by advisors. She must have been terrified as enemy armies marched toward the capital in 1814. When Paris fell and Napoléon was forced to abdicate in April 1814, Marie-Louise's *own* father, Emperor Francis, conveniently invited his daughter to bring little Napoléon II and come back home to Vienna. Napoléon, being sent to exile on the island of Elba, naively hoped Marie-Louise would join him or at least fight for their son's rights. But reality check: this was not Joséphine – there no ride-or-die devotion. Marie-Louise was a Habsburg princess to her core; when the chips were down, she stuck with her blood family. She took the toddler and left, effectively abandoning Napoléon to his fate.

Back in Austria, Marie-Louise was rewarded for her *dutiful betrayal*. The Treaty of Fontainebleau granted her the Duchy of Parma to rule, so she got a nice little *queendom* of her own in Italy. And here's the kicker: she promptly took up with an Austrian count, Adam von

Neipperg, who became her lover *almost immediately* (some say he was sent to "console" her – oh, he consoled her alright). By the time Napoléon escaped Elba and made his dramatic comeback for the Hundred Days in 1815, hoping maybe to reunite with his wife and son, Marie-Louise was entirely out of the picture. She didn't return to France, and she didn't send the baby either. Napoléon was definitively beaten at Waterloo, shipped off to exile on St. Helena, and Marie-Louise went on merrily to live in Parma with Neipperg, whom she married in 1821 after Napoléon died – having already had two children by him out of wedlock. Whew. If Joséphine was the wife who stayed loyal emotionally even after divorce, Marie-Louise was the wife who said "contract's over, bye!" as soon as the throne crumbled.

One can't help but appreciate the cosmic irony. Napoléon traded true love for a dynastic alliance and an heir. Yes, he got the heir – but the Empire fell apart anyway. And that heir, little Napoléon II, never ruled France; he grew up in Austria as a virtual prisoner of his grandfather, styled the Duke of Reichstadt, and died of illness at 21. So much for the grand dynastic dream. Napoléon himself later reportedly quipped, "I married a womb," reflecting that his calculation had been a cold one. The warm, witty Joséphine would famously not be around to comfort him in exile or to share in his final hours. Instead, Napoléon's final years on St. Helena were spent largely alone, with only memories (and a few loyal generals) for company.

Marriage Lesson: If you love her, don't dump her for an Austrian teenager

Napoléon Bonaparte's personal life played out like a tragicomic opera on the world stage. It's a story filled with passion, power, and paperwork (so much paperwork – those annulment documents!). And lurking underneath is a lesson as juicy as any reality TV moral: *all the power in the world can't replace the people you truly love.* Napoléon learned that the hard way. His final years in exile reveal a man haunted by choices. In 1814, while Napoléon was exiled on Elba, news reached him that Joséphine had died of pneumonia. The man who had faced down coalitions of kings was utterly shattered. He locked himself in his room and wept. "Josephine!" he cried out – her name on his lips even after their separation. In fact, when Napoléon himself lay dying on St. Helena in 1821, delirious and babbling, his last words are reputed to have been: *"France, the Army, the Head of the Army, Joséphine."* Even at the very end, he remembered his true love. One imagines Joséphine's ghost wagging a manicured finger and saying, "Shouldn't have let me go, Napy dear, shouldn't have let me go."

History has its own wicked sense of humor. The heir Napoléon secured by dumping Joséphine – that precious King of Rome – never sat on his father's throne. The Bourbon kings came back, and later, improbably, it was Joséphine's *grandson* who became Emperor as Napoléon III in 1852. Yes, through her first marriage, Joséphine was the grandmother of Napoleon III, as well as an ancestor of many European royals. In contrast, Napoléon's legitimate line with Marie-Louise vanished like a puff of smoke. In a way, Joséphine's blood returned to rule France, while Napoléon's dynastic gambit fizzled. Karma's a funny thing.

So, what lessons can we draw from this Napoleonic saga of love and power? Allow us to present a few timeless takeaways from Napoleon's Love Empire:

- Don't let Empire-sized ego wreck your romance: If you find yourself saying *"I adore my wife, but I need a younger model for an heir"*, slap yourself and reconsider. Napoléon's decision to put dynasty first left him with a big crown and an empty bed. Passionate letters are better than cold political contracts – just ask the guy who went from "constant object of my thoughts" to "dear political partner" in his correspondence.

- Midlife crisis decisions? Bad. Midlife crisis decisions that affect all of Europe? Worse: Napoléon swapping Joséphine for a teenager was basically a geopolitical midlife crisis. Sure, he got a son, but he also got a father-in-law who later joined his enemies. The in-laws from Austria were never going to truly be Team Napoléon. In the end, the rebound wife's family helped dethrone him. Let's call that #awkward.

- True love is irreplaceable (and will haunt you): Napoléon and Joséphine's bond, for all its messiness, was genuine. He never really got over her. The fact that "Joséphine" was on his lips with his dying breath says it all. Trading love for power is the ultimate devil's bargain – you might win a world, but you could lose your soul (or at least your happiness). If you're lucky enough to have a Joséphine, don't toss her aside for a Marie-Louise.

- Keep it amicable if you must part: To give credit, Napoléon and Joséphine set the gold standard for "conscious uncoupling" long before Gwyneth made it cool. They stayed friends

(Napoléon even sent Joséphine's granddaughter a wedding gift years after the divorce). They understood something modern celebs sometimes forget: you can end a marriage without ceasing to care. It's a small consolation, but it's something. Napolécn didn't lose Joséphine's love entirely; he carried it with him to the end.

In the grand soap opera of history, Napoléon's love life is a cautionary tale and a poignant drama all at once. It reminds us that even conquerors can get conquered by their own hearts. The next time you're flipping through a tabloid and see a headline about an older megastar leaving his loyal partner for a younger flame, you might whisper, "Don't do it! I read about Napoléon – it won't end well." After all, if you truly love her, don't dump her for an Austrian teenager. The price of that decision, as our dear Emperor learned, can be the loss of an *empire* and the love of your life. And those, mes amis, are two things not even a man who crowned himself can afford to lose.

Chapter 4

Royal Ruckus: Charles, Diana & Other Fairytale Fiascos

The Wedding Watched 'Round the World

Royal weddings never skimp on spectacle—just look at Charles and Diana's towering wedding cake above. But even that multi-tiered confection paled in comparison to the global hype for the "wedding of the century," as the July 29, 1981 nuptials of Prince Charles and Lady Diana Spencer were dubbed. It was a storybook set-up: the heir to the British throne and a shy 20-year-old kindergarten aide, poised to become a real-life princess in a puff-sleeved gown with a 25-foot train. An estimated 750 million people in 74 countries tuned in to watch the ceremony live—basically the Super Bowl of weddings (minus the nachos, plus a tiara). The whole world stopped for a moment, utterly enchanted by the grand St. Paul's Cathedral spectacle, the horse-drawn carriages, and the palpable promise of *happily ever after.*

Yet amid the fanfare, keen-eyed observers might have caught some foreshadowing more ominous than Lady Di's storm-cloud taffeta dress. During the couple's televised engagement interview, when asked if they were in love, Diana immediately replied "of course," while Charles famously quipped, "Whatever 'in love' means". (If that isn't a royal red flag, what is? Imagine a Bachelor finale where the guy proposes with "I guess I love you…whatever that means" – cue the collective cringe!). Diana later reportedly found that remark traumatizing, a sign that the fairy tale had some cracks in its veneer even before the vows. And speaking of vows, Diana *literally* stumbled over her prince's long list of names at the altar – calling him "Philip Charles Arthur George" instead of Charles Philip Arthur George – and pointedly omitted the word *"obey"* from her wedding oath. At the time, that omission caused a minor stir; in hindsight, it was the least revolutionary thing about this union.

Behind those iconic wedding photos of the beaming couple kissing on the Buckingham Palace balcony (a kiss that *sparked a new tradition*, since Charles forgot to kiss Diana at the altar in front of the Archbishop), real tensions were brewing. In the lead-up to the big day, both bride and groom had serious case of cold feet. Diana had discovered Charles had gifted a special bracelet to his former flame, Camilla Parker Bowles, just days before the wedding, leaving the naive 20-year-old distraught. She confided to her sisters that she seriously considered calling off the wedding – only to be told it was too late for that (the gown was fitted, the cake was iced, the world was watching… so down the aisle she went). Charles, for his part, was wracked with doubt as well: just hours before the ceremony, he was reportedly "confused and anxious," telling friends he felt *trapped by duty* – "I want to do the right thing by my country and my family," he said, even as he privately knew he and Diana had "nothing in common". In other words, the prince and princess were marching toward the altar with the enthusiasm of two people being gently prodded by Queen Elizabeth's prized corgis.

Of course, on the wedding day none of this drama was apparent to the public. To the millions watching, it looked like the grandest of fairy tales come to life. The bride was radiant (if a touch nervous, as she later admitted), the groom gallant, and the pomp and pageantry dialed up to eleven. As Diana glided up the aisle in her enormous ivory gown, she seemed every inch the Disney-esque princess – complete with glass coach and a glistening tiara. And when the newlyweds rode off in their carriage, waves and smiles on display, it was easy to believe in happily-ever-afters. But if this was a Disney movie, it was one directed by the makers of *Game of Thrones*. The audience got a sweeping romance, yes, but little did we know there were plot twists ahead involving a long-time mistress, public heartbreak, and enough royal scandal to fuel season after season of Netflix's "The Crown." The wedding may have been watched 'round the world, but soon the world would be watching the *marriage* – and that turned into a far less gilded spectacle.

Camilla, the Constant: Love Triangles in Buckingham

Every epic love triangle needs its third leg, and for Charles and Diana that was Camilla Parker Bowles – the woman who had been in Charles's life *before* and, fatefully, long *after* he said "I do." If Diana was the dazzling princess in this royal soap opera, Camilla often got cast as the sly villainess, lurking just offstage. Princess Di herself famously said, "there were three of us in this marriage, so it was a bit crowded". Ouch. Camilla was the enduring love of Charles's life – "the constant," as we might call her – and her shadow loomed large over the Wales's not-so-wedded bliss. In fact, Charles had first dated Camilla in the early 1970s, long before Diana came along, and they'd remained *close friends* (royal-speak for "totally still into each other") throughout Charles's courtship and marriage to Diana. By the mid-1980s, the prince had rekindled his romance with Camilla even though both were married with children at the time. It was the royal edition of *"Desperate Housewives"*, with castles and crowns replacing cul-de-sacs. And poor Diana – barely out of her teens and thrust onto the world stage – found herself in a real-life romantic rivalry that no amount of glass slippers could resolve.

The dynamics of this love triangle were messy to say the least. Diana grew increasingly suspicious and then certain of Charles's infidelity. By 1989, the normally demure princess had enough and *personally confronted Camilla* at a high-society birthday party. Can you imagine? The scene is practically scripted for a Netflix drama: Diana cornered Camilla and coolly said, *"I know what's going on between you and Charles and I just want you to know that."* Camilla, gutsy or perhaps in denial, replied, *"You've got everything you ever wanted. All the men in the world fall in love with you, and you've got two beautiful children, what more do you want?"* Diana didn't miss a beat: *"I want my husband,"* she shot back. Talk about a mic-drop moment – the People's Princess revealing her steel. Camilla had no real answer, and the two women parted, both shaken. It was an extraordinary, behind-closed-doors confrontation: the young princess and the prince's mistress facing off like a scene from *Dynasty*, but it was all too real. Diana later described herself as "terrified" of Camilla in that moment, but also felt a strange relief at finally speaking her truth. As she famously summed it up on TV later, that marriage was rather *"crowded"* indeed.

By the early 1990s, the royal dirty laundry was getting aired in public, and *boy* did it make headlines. In 1992, intimate "Camillagate" tapes were leaked, causing jaws to drop over breakfast tea across Britain. These were surreptitiously recorded phone calls between Charles and Camilla that confirmed their affair – including one cringe-inducing exchange involving Charles musing about wanting to be Camilla's tampon in another life (yes, really – the future King of England said that, and yes, it was that awkward). The press had a field day; you could practically hear the palace face-palming. That same year, Charles and Diana formally separated, announced on live TV by the Prime Minister as if it were a matter of state (because, in a way, it was). By 1994, Charles took the unprecedented step of admitting on national television that he had indeed been unfaithful with Camilla – an heir to the throne openly confessing adultery! – while Diana infamously dished about *her* own affair (with dashing cavalry officer James Hewitt) and the collapse of her marriage in a tell-all BBC interview. This was not your stiff-upper-lip, keep-calm-and-carry-on type of royal behavior. This was Messy Royal Scandal 101, unfolding in real time like a season of *The Crown* written by the folks at *Days of Our Lives.* And through it all, Camilla – the once private country wife – was vilified in the tabloids as the ultimate other woman. The British press, never known for subtlety, branded her with cruel nicknames. Diana herself reportedly referred to Camilla as "The Rottweiler," implying she was tenacious and, well, not particularly cute or cuddly. By the time Diana and Charles divorced in 1996, Camilla Parker Bowles had become arguably the most hated woman in Britain, unfairly *blamed by some for "breaking up the royal family"* and even for Diana's subsequent tragic death in 1997. Imagine being under that level of public hate – Camilla basically went into hiding in the late '90s, laying low while the world placed bouquets at Diana's gate and cast Camilla as a modern-day wicked stepmother in waiting.

And yet, fast forward a few years and the seemingly impossible happened: Charles and Camilla prevailed. They navigated the storm of public opinion, *very* slowly rehabilitated their images (a carefully managed PR campaign and a lot of time healed some wounds), and eventually, in 2005, the two finally married in a quiet civil ceremony. The one-time mistress became the Duchess of Cornwall, and later – with Queen Elizabeth II's passing and Charles's ascension – Camilla became Queen Consort, officially shedding the last traces of scandal to stand by Charles's side on the throne. Talk about a long game payoff! It's the kind of plot twist that would've sounded far-fetched even in a romance novel: the "other woman" ending up wearing the crown. Of course, the journey from pariah to popular acceptance wasn't exactly smooth. Even today, some Diana die-hards will forever side-eye Camilla. But public sentiment softened over the decades, and many Britons grudgingly came to accept that Charles's true love had always been Camilla. In an ironic way, Camilla was the constant in Charles's heart, outlasting a very turbulent marriage and decades of drama. The love triangle that once rocked Buckingham Palace resolved into a *pair* at the palace balcony. If there's a silver lining in this saga, perhaps it's that authenticity (eventually) won out: Charles ended up with the woman he loved, and Diana – who in life felt so trapped – became in memory an icon of independence and compassion. Still, the whole episode remains one of the juiciest royal fiascos of our time. And believe it or not, it wasn't even the first! For an even greater royal romantic uproar, we must flash back about 90 years to another Prince of Wales who fell head over heels... and nearly took the monarchy down with him.

Edward & Wallis: Abdicating for Affection

Long before Charles and Diana's marital melee, there was King Edward VIII and Wallis Simpson, the *OG* royal scandal that rocked the House of Windsor. This tale has all the makings of a Hollywood drama: a dashing king, a glamorous American divorcee, forbidden love, and the ultimate mic drop – the king giving up his throne for the woman he adored. It's the kind of story that would be *too implausible* if it weren't true. In 1936, King Edward VIII proved that even a king can get royally fed up with protocol. After less than a year on the throne, he declared that he simply couldn't continue being king without the "help and support of the woman I love". Yes, you read that right: he literally quit the top job in the kingdom for love. (Take *that*, fairy-tale trope of the commoner giving up everything to marry the prince – here the prince gave up being King!). Edward's heart belonged to Wallis Warfield Simpson, a stylish, twice-divorced American socialite with whom he'd been carrying on a very public love affair. For the hidebound British establishment of the 1930s, this was pure heresy. A British monarch *marrying* a divorced woman (let alone an American)? That was about as acceptable as, well, a British monarch abdicating – which is exactly what he did. Faced with a choice between the crown and his unconventional Cinderella, Edward chose Wallis. In a radio broadcast to a stunned nation, he explained, *"I have found it impossible to carry the heavy burden of responsibility...without the help and support of the woman I love."* Cue the collective gasps. It was a romantic gesture for the ages, or perhaps the ultimate act of royal recklessness – depending on whom you asked at the time.

The saga had everything: passion, scandal, and a constitutional crisis to top it all off. Government officials, church leaders, even Edward's own family were absolutely *aghast* at his determination to marry Wallis. As King, Edward was also the symbolic head of the Church of England, which in those days strictly forbade divorced people from remarrying in church if their ex-spouses were still alive. Wallis had not one but two living ex-husbands – a double no-no. The British tabloids (and there were plenty, even back then) gleefully painted Wallis as a cunning seductress leading the love-struck King astray. Some in the press whispered that she must have had "sinister charms" or ulterior motives – after all, what could *possibly* convince a man to give up an empire? Within the palace, courtiers fretted that Edward was "acting like a lovesick schoolboy." Prime Minister Stanley Baldwin basically told the King: *Wallis or the Crown – choose one.* And Edward, in a twist that upended centuries of royal tradition, chose Wallis. In December 1936, he signed the abdication papers, making him the only English sovereign ever to voluntarily abdicate the throne. Overnight, his stammering younger brother, Bertie (George VI), had to step up as King – a daunting job he hadn't asked for but performed admirably (if you've seen *The King's Speech*, you know the drill). As for Edward, he was demoted to Duke of Windsor and promptly whisked off into exile. In June 1937, he married Wallis in a small private ceremony in France – no big Westminster Abbey do, no adoring crowds, just two people in love tying the knot while the world looked on in shock and fascination.

The aftermath of this *royal romantic revolution* was complicated. Edward and Wallis became global celebrities of a sort – the paparazzi of the day followed their every move as they trotted around Europe and the U.S., hobnobbing with high society and even some unsavory political figures (their friendly visit with Hitler in 1937 – yes, *that* Hitler – remains a permanent stain on their reputations, proving that love doesn't necessarily make you a great judge of character). The former King – once Emperor of India and Head of the Commonwealth – spent the rest of his life essentially as a stylish socialite, hosting parties in Paris, golfing, and writing memoirs. Wallis, now the Duchess of Windsor, became a fashion icon known for her chic style and biting wit (she's often credited with quipping, "You can never be too rich or too thin," an ethos she seemed to live by). They had money, glamour, and each other, but they lived perpetually in the shadow of the monarchy they left behind. The royal family mostly shunned them; Queen Mary (Edward's mother) never forgave her son, and Wallis was pointedly not invited to many family events. The Duke and Duchess of Windsor were effectively the *original* royal reality show stars, famous for who they were more than any meaningful things they did post-abdication. There was always an air of scandal about them – as late as the 1960s, Wallis's very presence could set tongues wagging at Buckingham Palace.

Yet, through all the drama and exile, Edward and Wallis stayed together until his death in 1972, proving that his shocking sacrifice was, at least, not in vain. They were a love match, unquestionably, albeit one that came at a stupendous cost. The British monarchy, for its part, survived this near-knockout blow and learned a few lessons. Edward's abdication inadvertently paved the way for his niece,

Elizabeth II, to become one of the greatest queens in history. (Small irony: had Edward not abdicated, "Lilibet" might never have worn the crown, and the last 70 years of royal history would look very different – not to mention *The Crown* would have needed a whole new plot!). In public memory, Edward and Wallis's tale is a mix of romance and cautionary tale: a glamorous lark that forced the royals to modernize… slowly. It's a story so juicy and dramatic that it's been retold endlessly in books, movies, and TV – because who doesn't love a *good* "royal gives up everything for love" saga? If Charles and Diana's implosion was the biggest royal fiasco of the late 20th century, Edward and Wallis's abdication was the granddaddy of all fairytale fiascos – a reminder that sometimes the crown and the heart just don't ride off into the sunset together.

Marriage Lesson: Even Royalty Needs Therapy—And Better Prenups

What have we learned from this cavalcade of crown-clad couple chaos? First off, that even the most exalted royals are, at the end of the day, as human as the rest of us – prone to heart-eyes and heartbreak, swept up in passion, mired in regret. The difference is when *their* love lives go off the rails, it's like watching a high-speed train wreck in full public view, with palace spokespeople and prime ministers making announcements, and Netflix eventually green-lighting a series about it. If there's a silver lining, it's the reassurance that no one is immune to relationship struggles. Billion-dollar palace? Check. Gold coach and crown? Check. Emotional baggage and communication issues? Check and check. It turns out a title of "Prince" or "Princess" doesn't come with a magic wand to wave away marital woes. In fact, the pressures of royal life – the duty, the public scrutiny, the expectations to produce "an heir and a spare" on schedule – seem to amplify the stress on these marriages. (One might argue Henry VIII could have saved himself six marriages and a few headless former spouses *if only he'd had a good couples counselor on call.*) Modern royals, thankfully, are more likely to seek help than send their wives to the chopping block. Even Charles and Diana, back in the '80s, tried marriage counseling; the Queen reportedly brought in a therapist, Dr. Alan McGlashan, to help the warring Waleses. Diana wasn't keen on the sessions and bowed out, but Charles continued seeing the therapist solo for 14 years – proof that even princes need someone to talk to. Perhaps if both had fully engaged in therapy, history might have gone differently… or at least been a tad less acrimonious. Which brings us to lesson one: even royalty needs therapy. Stiff upper lip be darned – a good therapist might have done wonders in untangling the emotional mess that was Charles and Diana's union, or helped Edward VIII think through the long-term fallout of abdication beyond "love conquers all." Consider this: in a world where princes and princesses actually worked through their issues privately on a therapist's couch, we might have had far fewer "fairytale fiascos" to gossip about (but then what would the tabloids do for headlines?).

Lesson two: get a better prenup (or any prenup at all). Royals traditionally don't do prenuptial agreements – it's not exactly the romantic, storybook thing to slide across the table along with the engagement ring. But given the *astronomical stakes* of royal divorces, maybe they should start. When Charles and Diana split, the settlement was hefty – Diana walked away with a reported £17 million lump sum plus £400,000 a year (and that was in 1996 money, enough to make any aristocratic accountant break into a cold sweat). Not to mention the cost to the monarchy's reputation from all the mud-slinging that accompanied their breakup. If a solid prenup had been in place, perhaps some of the ugliness (and expense) could've been mitigated – or even better, the sheer act of discussing a prenup might force a couple to confront tough issues *before* walking down the aisle. And speaking of costly breakups, let's not forget poor Britain nearly had a constitutional collapse over Edward and Wallis. A prenup wouldn't have saved that (the issue was love vs. throne, not money), but one can't help but think the House of Windsor could use an HR department and a legal team as much as it uses matchmakers. After all, when commoners divorce, they fight over who gets the house; when royals divorce, they fret over who gets to keep the *HRH style* and which palaces the ex gets to live in. A little forward planning couldn't hurt.

Finally, perhaps the biggest lesson is a humble one: royalty – they're just like us, only with more sparkly accessories. Fairy tale narratives are nice for the tourism brochures, but real marriages (even royal ones) take work, compromise, and maybe a dose of *reality* not often found in palace protocols. The tales of Charles and Diana, and Edward and Wallis, explode the myth of the perfect prince and princess riding into the sunset. In truth, the royal castle can feel like a gilded cage when love is AWOL. All the titles and tiaras in the world won't guarantee a happy union – that requires honesty, compatibility, and sometimes doing the hard, un-glamorous work (again, therapy!). And if those things are lacking, no amount of pomp and circumstance can paper it over for long. The British Royal Family has modernized with each fiasco – however painfully. Charles's generation saw the acceptance of marrying for love (even if it took a roundabout route);

Edward VIII's scandal indirectly ushered in a more humble, duty-first monarchy under George VI and Elizabeth II. Today, we see princes marrying former actresses, and princesses speaking openly about mental health – unthinkable in Edward's time. Progress! Even so, the Crown has a way to go in the love department. Perhaps future royals will read this chapter in their history and take heed: marry someone you truly connect with, seek help when you need it, and maybe have the lawyers draft a little something *just in case*. Because if there's one thing these "fairytale fiascos" have shown, it's that *happily ever after* isn't guaranteed – not even if you live in a palace.

So, the next time you find yourself envying the prince or princess's life, remember the Royal Ruckus behind those palace doors. From Charles and Diana's shattered happily-ever-after to Edward and Wallis's throne-shaking romance, royal love stories often come with more drama than a season finale of *The Real Housewives*. They're cautionary tales wrapped in ermine. Even royalty needs a reality check (and maybe a good counselor). In the end, the crown may be heavy, but matters of the heart are heavier – whether you're a commoner or a king. And that, dear reader, is the *real* tea on fairytale fiascos. Cheers to love, and may all our romances – royal or not – have a bit more sense (and much less scandal) than those of our befuddled blue-blooded friends.

Chapter 5

Tinseltown Tango: Hollywood's Glamour & Greasepaint

Welcome to Tinseltown, where love isn't just in the air – it's scripted in neon and written in scandalous headlines. In Hollywood's golden age, romance came drenched in glamour and greasepaint, playing out like a high-drama tango under klieg lights. Our stage features legendary couples whose passionate love affairs and marital implosions had more plot twists than a blockbuster melodrama. Grab your popcorn as we dish on three classic Hollywood romances – and wreckages – with all the wit and whimsy of a gossip columnist who's seen it all.

Liz & Dick: Love, Take One and Two

Elizabeth "Liz" Taylor and Richard "Dick" Burton weren't just Hollywood royalty – they were the original blockbuster couple who turned their own lives into a sizzling soap opera. The two megastars met on the set of *Cleopatra* in 1962 in full ancient regalia, where Burton's first cheesy pickup line to Taylor was, "Has anybody ever told you that you're a very pretty girl?". (Cue eye roll from Liz – she quipped, "Oy gevalt… here's the great lover… and he comes out with a line like that".) Despite the rocky start, their on-set chemistry as Antony and Cleopatra sparked an inferno of love and lust that could be seen from space. Both were married to others at the time, and when their torrid affair became public it created an international sensation. How sensational? Try *paparazzi origin story*-level sensational. A sneaky photographer snapped the couple canoodling on a yacht in Italy, igniting a scandal so big even the Vatican felt compelled to chime in – condemning Taylor for "erotic vagrancy". (When a love affair draws fire from the Pope and Congress debates banning you from the country, you know you've made tabloid history.)

Dubbed "Liz and Dick" by breathless columnists, Taylor and Burton embraced the drama they'd created. In 1964, after divorcing their respective spouses, they married in a lavish ceremony – Liz's fifth trip down the aisle, but who's counting? Thus began a rollercoaster union fueled by fame, fights, and fabulous jewels. The pair made 11 films together, and everywhere they went a media circus followed.

One moment they'd be exchanging swoony love notes; the next, hurling insults (or glassware) across a five-star hotel suite. They drank and bickered with Shakespearean flair – small wonder they won acclaim playing the battling spouses of *Who's Afraid of Virginia Woolf?*, as life imitated art. Burton showered Taylor with extravagant gifts as grand as their egos – including a 69-carat diamond the size of a jawbreaker – because, as Liz famously said, "Big girls need big diamonds." When things were good, they were larger-than-life: jet-setting on yachts, dripping with gems, inspiring headlines that made ordinary newlyweds look positively boring.

But when things went bad, the fireworks were equally epic. Both were notoriously jealous and hot-tempered, and their blowups were the stuff of Hollywood legend. (Example: during one film shoot, Liz allegedly caught Dick getting too cozy with a young actress. Never one to underplay a scene, Taylor literally leapt out from behind a sofa, brandishing a broken vodka bottle, and chased the startled starlet off the set. Hell hath no fury like Liz with a liquor bottle in hand.) Over the years, the constant "drunk in love" routine took its toll: TVs were smashed, promises broken, and their once fairy-tale romance started to look more like a Tennessee Williams drama. By 1974, after a decade of turmoil, the legendary lovers finally called it quits and divorced.

In true Hollywood fashion, that wasn't the end of the story. Like a blockbuster film spawning an unexpected sequel, Liz and Dick couldn't resist a comeback. In 1975 they remarried for "Take Two" of their love story – only to divorce *again* less than a year later. (What can we say, the sequel rarely lives up to the original.) A drained Elizabeth Taylor confessed afterward, "I don't want to be that much in love ever again… I gave everything away – my soul, my being, everything," she told a friend.

Indeed, their passion burned so white-hot it practically vaporized. Yet for all the public blowouts and tabloid fodder, Liz and Dick maintained a profound, if turbulent, bond. "When you are in love and lust like that," Taylor reflected, "you just grab it with both hands and ride out the storm" – and ride it out they did, through roaring fights and radiant makeups, until there was nothing left to burn. Still, the Liz & Dick saga left an indelible mark on Hollywood romance. They showed that sometimes love *can* conquer all – except maybe itself. Their tango was as dazzling as it was destructive, equal parts glamour and greasepaint. And if you thought *that* was dramatic, wait till you see how another blonde goddess and her Yankee prince fared in the marital ring…

Marilyn & Joe: A Curveball Marriage

Marilyn Monroe and Joe DiMaggio seemed like a storybook pairing on paper – America's favorite blonde bombshell and the Yankee Clipper himself, a baseball hero. It was the kind of matchup a studio PR agent would dream up: Beauty marries Baseball in an all-American romance. They tied the knot in January 1954 in a low-key City Hall ceremony (Marilyn wore a demure brown suit instead of a gown, as if to say this was a sensible marriage, not a Hollywood fling). Fans mobbed them in the street, cheering for this union of Hollywood glamour and athletic stardom. The press ate it up, billing them as a real-life fairy tale: the slugger and the starlet. But once the confetti settled, Marilyn and Joe discovered that a fairy tale coupling between a Hollywood diva and a traditional ballplayer might be destined for a fizzle ending – a real curveball, if you will.

From the get-go, their marriage was a clash of worlds. Marilyn was a free-spirited sex symbol at the peak of her fame – a woman who *literally* made subway grates sizzle. Joe, on the other hand, was a straight-laced, proud ex-athlete who expected a conventional wife well away from the spotlight. He was ready to retire to private life; she was chasing bigger movie roles and respect as an actress. DiMaggio had been entranced by Marilyn's glamour from afar, but up close he struggled with it. Rumors later abounded that he was intensely jealous and didn't like that he had to "share her with the rest of the world". In truth, Joe wanted Marilyn to be more Mrs. DiMaggio, less global bombshell; Marilyn, ever the star, just couldn't dim her light. That tension came to a head – famously – on September 15, 1954, during the filming of *The Seven Year Itch*. As Marilyn stood over a New York subway grate, the updraft sent her white skirt billowing high, creating an iconic, cheeky movie moment. The gathered crowd roared its approval, camera bulbs flashed... and Joe DiMaggio's face turned to thunder. To the public, it was a fun bit of movie magic; to Joe, it was his wife "exhibiting" herself in front of leering strangers. The scene infuriated him, and the couple had a ferocious argument that night – a fight loud enough to be heard through their hotel walls, if legend is to be believed. It proved a breaking point. Not long after that infamous flying-skirt incident, Marilyn filed for divorce, citing "mental cruelty" in the official papers. Their marriage had lasted just nine months – barely longer than a Yankees winning streak.

Hollywood gossip columns went into overdrive. How could the world's most desirable woman and baseball's biggest icon not make it work for even a year? The answer, in hindsight, seems obvious: Marilyn and Joe wanted completely different things. She craved freedom, creative fulfillment, and, yes, the adoration of millions of fans; he craved a homey domesticity that didn't involve his wife's skirt flying up for the cameras. She lived for the spotlight, he winced from it. Neither could play second fiddle, so their duet quickly turned into a solo act. Marilyn later admitted they were "too far apart in our beliefs," and friends observed that Joe simply couldn't handle Marilyn being a sex symbol for the world rather than just for him. A traditional guy from a conservative background, DiMaggio saw his wife's provocative stardom as a personal affront, while Marilyn couldn't conform to the role of obedient housewife. Their love was real (the shy Joe had pursued Marilyn ardently, and she was charmed by his old-fashioned gallantry), but their lifestyles were a bad mismatch from day one.

Yet Joe and Marilyn's story didn't end with the divorce decree – and here's where it takes a turn that could thaw even a cynical heart. In the years after their split, Joe's love for Marilyn in some ways *grew*. He watched from afar as she remarried (to playwright Arthur Miller) and later struggled through career and personal troubles. When Marilyn's world started spiraling – her health faltering, her confidence shaky – Joe quietly stepped back into her life as a friend and protector. After her divorce from Miller, it was Joe who supported Marilyn during a rough patch, reportedly even planning to remarry her. Tragically, Marilyn Monroe's tumultuous life was cut short in August 1962. DiMaggio took charge of her funeral arrangements, fiercely shielding her dignity from the Hollywood circus.

And in perhaps one of the most achingly romantic gestures of all time, the heartbroken Joe began sending roses to Marilyn's grave – not once, but three times a week – and he kept it up for twenty years. He never remarried. According to his lawyer, on Joe's own deathbed decades later, his final whispered words were, "I'll finally get to see Marilyn". If their marriage was a strikeout, Joe's enduring devotion became the stuff of legend. In a Hollywood plot twist, the baseball star best known for hitting streaks turned out to be a true romantic lead after all – albeit too late for a happily ever after.

Ava & Frank: High Notes and Low Blows

When sultry screen siren Ava Gardner fell for crooner Frank Sinatra, it was a match made in tabloid heaven – and occasionally, hell. Picture it: Frank "Ol' Blue Eyes" Sinatra, the Italian-American music idol with a bad-boy streak, and Ava Gardner, the North Carolina farm girl turned Hollywood goddess so gorgeous that her second husband Artie Shaw called her "the most beautiful creature you ever saw".

Gardner also had a "reckless streak and an insatiable appetite for booze and boys" – the kind of gal who could out-party a Rat Packer. Sparks were inevitable when these two got together. They met in the late 1940s while Sinatra was still married to his childhood sweetheart Nancy, but that didn't stop the flirtation. By 1951, Frank had left Nancy and married Ava, and the press had a field day. Ava was marrying for the third time (she'd already collected two ex-husbands), Frank was in a career slump and fresh off a scandalous divorce – it was the perfect Hollywood narrative: the bad-boy singer and the femme fatale, riding off into the sunset amid equal parts adoration and finger-wagging.

For a while, the glamour of "Frank and Ava" was undeniable. They were young, beautiful, and madly in love – the kind of passionate love that inspires torch songs and smashed champagne glasses. On their honeymoon, paparazzi hounded them relentlessly; the two couldn't even stroll a beach barefoot without flashbulbs popping (a frustrated Ava vented that "the world wouldn't leave us alone for a second"). But even away from cameras, peace wasn't easy for this volatile duo. Both Frank and Ava were, by Ava's own admission, "high-strung people, possessive and jealous and liable to explode fast". When Ava lost her temper, "honey, you can't find it anyplace," she said – and Frank was the same way. Their fights were as legendary as their affection. Neighbors and hotel guests likely felt they got a free show whenever these two went at it: shouting matches, tears, dramatic exits. One fight famously saw Sinatra hurl a wine bottle (some say it was a champagne bottle) out a window; in another notorious spat, he allegedly threw a water-filled douche bag at Ava and her friend Lana Turner (talk about a low blow – Frank's aim was as bold as his lyrics).

Yet just as fiercely as they fought, they loved. The make-up sessions between Frank and Ava were the stuff of spicy Hollywood lore (whispers of days spent sequestered in hotel suites, reconciling in the most… ahem… enthusiastic ways).

Amid this stormy sea of passion, their individual lives were in upheaval too. Ava's film career was skyrocketing – by the early '50s she was a bona fide star – while Frank's popularity had hit the skids. He'd been dropped by his record label and was desperate for a big acting role to revive his fortunes. This power imbalance could have sunk them (Hollywood has a way of bruising the male ego when the Mrs. is more successful), but credit Ava for literally saving Frank's career. When the role of Maggio in *From Here to Eternity* came up – a part that would become Frank's big comeback – Ava championed her husband. She lobbied the studio boss on Frank's behalf and helped convince him to give Frank a shot. Ultimately, Sinatra landed the role, and in 1954 he won an Academy Award for it, marking one of Hollywood's great comeback stories. For a brief golden moment, the Sinatras were on top of the world together, celebrating his triumph in style (they toasted his Oscar in an African safari camp while Ava was on location for *Mogambo*).

But a Hollywood story this juicy demands a fall – and fall it did. No sooner had Frank regained his fame than the marriage began unraveling. The same jealousy and volatility that fueled their passion also sowed chaos. Both had wandering eyes (their mutual infidelities were an open secret), and the explosive confrontations kept coming. By late 1953, just two years after they wed, Ava and Frank had separated, and in 1954 they announced plans to divorce. (The legal divorce wouldn't be final until 1957, but their marriage was effectively over long before.) Sinatra was devastated; he reportedly attempted suicide multiple times over their breakup, unable to imagine life without Ava. He poured his heartbreak into music, recording the soulful album *In the Wee Small Hours* – a classic drenched in loneliness that many say was inspired by losing Ava.

As for Ava, she later called Frank the love of her life, saying they would be "lovers forever – eternally," even after parting ways. Indeed, though divorced, the two never fully let go of each other. They remained close friends and occasional lovers, sneaking off for secret reunions across the globe in the years that followed. And when Sinatra, at age 50, impulsively married 21-year-old Mia Farrow in 1966, Ava delivered one of her famously tart one-liners: "I always knew Frank would wind up in bed with a boy," she smirked, still the one woman who could make Ol' Blue Eyes turn red.

Ava and Frank's love story was messy, melodramatic, and absolutely drenched in Old Hollywood glamour – a true tango of high notes and low blows. They taught each other about passion and pain in equal measure. In the end, their marriage couldn't survive the tempest of two outsized personalities, but it left an imprint on both of them that lasted a lifetime. Frank never quite got over Ava – you can hear the lingering heartache in his most plaintive ballads – and Ava, for all her later adventures, kept a soft spot for the skinny singer who had stolen her heart.

Marriage Lesson: Don't Cast Your Spouse as a Supporting Actor in Your Personal Drama

What grand lesson can we draw from these over-the-top romances, besides the obvious ("maybe *don't* marry eight times, Liz")? If there's one thing these Hollywood love stories illustrate, it's that a marriage can't have just one star. In the movies, someone plays the lead and someone the supporting role – but in a real-life partnership, treating your spouse like a bit player in *your* drama is a recipe for an unhappy ending. Liz Taylor, Marilyn Monroe, and Ava Gardner were each supernovas in their own right – women of immense talent, beauty, and yes, ego – and they married men who weren't exactly shrinking violets themselves. Each couple's implosion came, in part, from a battle of spotlights: whose career, whose needs, whose ego would get top billing?

Consider Liz and Dick: two Oscar-winning egos sharing the same frame. They loved each other deeply, but they also each expected to be the center of attention. When both spouses demand the lead role, the script veers toward chaos (and occasionally vodka-bottle sword fights). Similarly, Marilyn and Joe's brief union was doomed by mismatched expectations – Joe wanted a wife who would step out of the limelight, Marilyn was a superstar who *lived* in it. Neither could bear a supporting role, so their duet turned into a quick solo. And Ava and Frank? They were like two divas trying to sing a duet with each belting in a different key – thrilling in small doses, but unsustainable as a full-length performance.

The takeaway: even in a town built on make-believe, you can't *fake* a balanced relationship. A successful marriage needs compromise and co-starring credits for both parties. The Hollywood couples of yesteryear often learned this the hard way. Instead of an equal partner, each spouse got a rival or a rescuer, and the plot of their lives careened off course. Perhaps if Burton had been content to let Elizabeth shine without feeling threatened, or if DiMaggio could have embraced Marilyn's stardom rather than resenting it, things might have ended differently. But then, where would the drama be? (And let's face it, we secretly love the drama.)

So, dear reader, if you ever find yourself waltzing through a high-stakes tango of love, remember the wisdom gleaned from Tinseltown's trials and tribulations. Share the spotlight – it's big enough for two – and don't script your spouse into a bit part. Otherwise, you might end up giving the performance of your life in divorce court, wondering where it all went wrong. Better to learn from these glamorous cautionary tales: keep the love real, keep the egos in check, and save the greasepaint for the movies. After all, when it comes to happily ever after, it takes two stars in harmony to truly steal the show.

Chapter 6

Rock 'n' Roll Romances:
Juke-Box Couplings

Elvis & Priscilla: Hound Dog Days

Once upon a time in rock 'n' roll, the King found his queen – or rather, a 14-year-old schoolgirl who caught his eye at an Army base. Yes, Elvis Presley met Priscilla Beaulieu in 1959 while stationed in Germany, and he was instantly lovestruck. If Twitter had existed, the outrage would've melted the internet faster than Elvis could swivel his hips. But in the late '50s, this courtship was hush-hush. Priscilla's parents, initially aghast, struck a deal: they let their daughter move to Graceland at 17 on the condition that Elvis eventually *put a ring on it*. So, Priscilla moved into a life of pink Cadillacs and peanut-butter-and-banana sandwiches, essentially becoming the teen queen of Graceland under the King's careful watch. Elvis, ever the Southern gentleman (with a twist of "Jailhouse Rock" rebellion), made sure Priscilla went to school by day – but all bets were off by night. As Priscilla later quipped, she was *"a schoolgirl by day, femme fatale by night"* living at Graceland. This was less a conventional romance and more like a rock star's DIY finishing school for his future bride.

Elvis finally made good on the promise in 1967. The wedding was the stuff of tabloid dreams and comedic legend: a Las Vegas ceremony at the Aladdin Hotel that lasted all of eight minutes. (Dearly beloved, we are gathered – and *boom*, they were married before the chapel organist could finish a verse of "Love Me Tender.") Colonel Tom Parker, Elvis's shrewd manager, orchestrated the quickie ceremony with military precision to avoid a media circus. After all, Elvis was the biggest star on the planet – think *Justin Timberlake, Harry Styles, and a dash of Brad Pitt rolled into one pompadoured package*. Keeping this wedding under wraps was like trying to hide an elephant in a phone booth. Yet they pulled it off: 14 guests, a $3,200 cake (that's about $22,000 today, because even the cake had to be fit for a King), and a 9:00 a.m. champagne breakfast with the press corps invited *after* the vows. Elvis even had the word "obey" removed from the vows – a king knows he's not taking orders. In photos, the newlyweds were all smiles, cutting that six-tier cake and toasting with bubbly as if to say, "Here's to a normal married life, thank you very much."

For a while, Elvis and Priscilla played house in high style. They soon welcomed a daughter, Lisa Marie, exactly nine months after the wedding (Elvis may have been a rebel, but he had excellent timing). The world swooned over this picture-perfect rock 'n' roll family – Elvis, the once-snarling "Hound Dog" singer, now changing diapers at Graceland. But domestic life was *not* all blue suede and roses. By the late '60s, Elvis's career was shifting (the '68 Comeback Special loomed) and so were his habits. He kept nocturnal hours that turned Priscilla's daily routine upside down, and he had a penchant for *sharing his love* a little too freely on the road. (Let's just say Elvis's wandering eye made him less faithful than his iconic hairstyle – that slick pompadour never moved, but Elvis certainly did.) Priscilla later admitted that Elvis was "with other women" throughout their relationship, dalliances ranging from Hollywood co-stars to adoring fans. The King's castle, it turned out, had many side doors.

Priscilla, for her part, tried to mold herself into Elvis's ideal. He chose her outfits, her hairstyles, even had her get her teeth capped – creating his own living doll. For a while, she went along with it, the loyal queen to the King. But as the "Hound Dog days" wore on, Priscilla grew restless. She found passions of her own – like karate, of all things. (When your husband is out late *Suspicious Minds*-ing, why not take up karate to kick the boredom?) In 1972, Priscilla's karate instructor, Mike Stone, became more than just a teacher. Priscilla fell for him and ultimately confessed to Elvis she was leaving. The King did *not* take this well – legend has it he flew into a rage, at one point suggesting a hitman for Mike before cooler heads prevailed. You could say Elvis was *"all shook up"* in the worst way. The marriage had hit the rocks, and no amount of heartfelt ballads could save it.

By 1973, it was officially over – Elvis and Priscilla divorced after six years of marriage. In true bizarre celebrity fashion, they exited the courthouse hand in hand and even shared a friendly kiss for cameras on divorce day. (Nothing says "amicable" like canoodling *after* signing the divorce papers – a moment so surreal it could make a soap opera writer blush.) Priscilla walked away with a chunk of Elvis's fortune and custody of Lisa Marie, and Elvis walked into the Las Vegas sunset of the 1970s, resplendent in sequined jumpsuits and tragic loneliness. He told reporters they were still friends, and indeed Priscilla remained one of Elvis's closest confidantes until his death in 1977. It's as if they couldn't quit the habit of caring for each other, even when the marriage had left the building.

The Elvis-Priscilla saga set the template for rock 'n' roll romances: *a meteoric start, a melodramatic middle, and an ending equal parts heartbreaking and absurd.* It had all the ingredients of a VH1 special – scandal, true love, deception, and a touch of kitsch (not to mention a literal King and his teenage queen). Their story proved that even rock royalty isn't immune to the mundane pains of love. As Elvis might say, *they couldn't help falling in love*, but staying in love was a different song and dance. And so, with the King back on the singles chart (in life, if not on Billboard), we turn the record to another famous couple who belted out a tune of togetherness – until life remixed it. If Elvis and Priscilla were a rock fairy tale, the next duo gives us a technicolor pop sitcom that morphed into a courtroom drama.

Sonny & Cher: I Got You, Then I Didn't

Meet Sonny and Cher, the swinging '60s couple who practically invented the celebrity duet. These two started as a bohemian Bonnie and Clyde – only with cooler hair and a better soundtrack. Salvatore "Sonny" Bono was a 28-year-old music industry gofer-turned-songwriter when he met Cherilyn Sarkisian in an L.A. coffee shop in 1962. She was just 16, a high school dropout with starry eyes and a voice like honey. Their origin story reads like a Hollywood rom-com: Cher needed a place to crash; Sonny gallantly offered his spare bed (platonically, at first – he supposedly said, *"I don't find you particularly attractive"* when she moved in). But love bloomed to the sound of *Phil Spector's* roaring Wall of Sound. Soon Cher was singing backup on tracks like "Be My Baby," and by 1965 the duo had a new name – Sonny & Cher – and a smash hit "I Got You Babe." They weren't just singing about young love; they were living it, complete with fur vests, bell-bottoms, and hippie wedding rings engraved with each other's names.

Publicly, Sonny and Cher were the *adorably mismatched sweethearts* of the late '60s. He was short, she was tall. He was the goofy straight man; she was the deadpan zinger with a megawatt smile. Together, they exuded a playful marital harmony that America ate up like candy. By the early '70s, they'd parlayed that image into "The Sonny & Cher Comedy Hour," a prime-time variety show where they wisecracked and warbled in equal measure. Every week, families tuned in to see Sonny get gently roasted by Cher's one-liners (*"Sonny's idea of a partnership is he doesn't work and I make the money,"* she'd quip while he rolled his eyes). They bickered on stage in a way that felt real and relatable – a bit like *Lucy and Ricky* for the flower-power generation. Viewers assumed that behind the scenes, they were just as devoted as in their signature love anthem *"I Got You Babe."* For a while, that was true: they had a daughter, Chastity, in 1969 and were the poster couple of funky, egalitarian love.

But oh, *the times, they were a-changin'*. By 1974, the harmony was way off-key. Off camera, Cher later revealed, Sonny had become an overbearing Svengali – controlling every aspect of her life and career. He kept her working endlessly; he managed the money (not always in Cher's favor, as she'd find out); he even dictated her social life. *"I wasn't allowed to do anything except work. We worked more than we lived,"* Cher said, looking back. To make matters worse, Sonny was a philanderer of epic proportions – the mustachioed Romeo couldn't resist the lure of groupies and starlets. *"Stardom made Sonny a huge womanizer. One woman, or even five, was not enough for him,"* Cher quipped, probably with a sardonic eyebrow raise. She was faithful; he was not. The duo that sang *"I got you"* was falling apart because Sonny seemingly had *everyone* else too. In true Hollywood fashion, they kept up appearances longer than they should have – their variety show continued even as they privately separated. By 1974, the cracks were visible. The banter on TV got a little too pointed, the smiles a little too forced. Audiences didn't know it yet, but they were essentially watching a marriage implode in real time with a laugh track.

Cher finally had enough. In 1974 she dropped a bombshell, filing for divorce and citing *"involuntary servitude"* as the cause. (Yes, she literally accused Sonny of making her his indentured servant – a legal zinger that stunned the industry.) It turned out Sonny had signed Cher into a horrendous business contract – she effectively *worked for him*, owned none of their assets, and even her stage name was under his control. When Cher's pal David Geffen reviewed the paperwork, he told her it was the worst one-sided contract he'd ever seen. The ensuing divorce battle was about as pretty as Sonny's polyester suits. They fought over money, over the custody of little Chastity, and over TV contracts. The tabloids went wild – *America's favorite couple splits!* It was as if Donny and Marie Osmond announced a cage fight. People were shocked that the duo who serenaded each other so lovingly could turn so bitter. But behind closed doors, Cher was reclaiming her freedom and Sonny was scrambling to maintain the image (and income stream) he'd built around their marriage.

The divorce was finalized in 1975, and the Sonny & Cher show was no more. In a strange epilogue, they each got their own TV variety shows (because the best way to get over a breakup is to split your shared audience). Cher, ever the superstar, shone on her solo show with bold costumes and that famous swagger. Sonny's solo attempt... well, let's just say the world didn't exactly demand *The Sonny Bono Hour*. Perhaps the wildest twist came *after* the ink dried on the divorce: Cher, in true rock 'n' roll fashion, married another man just *days* later. She fell into the arms of Gregg Allman of the Allman Brothers Band, a long-haired Southern rock prince, and tied the knot *three days* after ditching Sonny. If that sounds impulsive, it was. Nine days into the Allman marriage, Cher was like "Oops, never mind" and filed for divorce from him too. (Apparently, Gregg's volatile mix of heroin and alcohol made for a lousy honeymoon – who could've guessed?) That union did stagger on a bit longer after a reconciliation – they even had a child together – but it fizzled by 1979. Cher was now 0 for 2 in the celebrity marriage arena, proving that even a goddess of pop can't catch a break in love.

And what of Sonny? In a plot twist no one saw coming, he went from hippie pop icon to U.S. Congressman in the '90s. (Truly, the 1960s were a hell of a drug.) He and Cher did patch up their friendship eventually. In 1987, over a decade after their split, they famously reunited on David Letterman's stage for an impromptu duet of "I Got You Babe," giving everyone the warm fuzzies and a strange sense of closure. By then, the once inseparable duo had gone down radically different paths. Cher became an Oscar-winning, chart-topping icon who turned back time in a thong bodysuit, while Sonny donned a suit and went off to make laws (and, sadly, met an untimely end in a skiing accident in 1998).

The Sonny & Cher saga was like a vintage tabloid column come to life: wholesome enchantment followed by soap-operatic unraveling. It carried the ironic lesson that singing "I got you" at the top of your lungs doesn't guarantee you'll *keep* each other. They rode the charts together and crashed apart spectacularly, all in the public eye. If their love story had a soundtrack, Side A was sunny California pop and Side B was a courtroom blues. Yet, cultural significance abounds – they embodied the ideal of free-spirited '60s love, then their breakup became a cautionary tale of mixing business, fame, and marriage. As Cher herself noted later, "We had a weird relationship. I don't expect anybody to understand it". Weird as it was, we all *felt* like we understood – because in the end, theirs was a human story of love found, lost, and survived. And so, with the final notes of "I Got You Babe" echoing into history, we turn to a rock romance that took intra-band drama to new heights (and lows). If one celebrity couple's split is messy, wait till you see a whole band's love lives go up in flames simultaneously.

Fleetwood Fights: When Bandmates Marry and Battle

Every band has *some* drama, but Fleetwood Mac said, "Hold our beer and hand us our guitars." The British-American rock outfit turned their romantic entanglements into a multiplatinum masterpiece and a soap opera with the greatest soundtrack ever. Picture a late-1970s recording studio in California: five band members, two separate couples on the rocks, a dash of extra-marital intrigue, mountains of cocaine, and enough heartbreak to fuel a dozen breakup albums. Instead, all that drama got distilled into one: the 1977 classic *Rumours*. It's the album that gave us "Go Your Own Way" and "Dreams" – essentially musical subtweets between ex-lovers – and it was created amid relationship chaos so intense it's a wonder they didn't all quit to join a monastery.

Let's set the stage. By 1976, Lindsey Buckingham (the lead guitarist) and Stevie Nicks (the mystical queen of rock) were a long-term couple whose love had curdled into resentment. Across the room, Christine McVie (keyboardist and songwriter) and John McVie (bassist) were married – and *not* happily. In fact, Christine and John were in the middle of a divorce while the band was making *Rumours*. Oh, and the band's namesake drummer, Mick Fleetwood, was busy discovering his wife had cheated *on him*, and would soon embark on an affair *with Stevie Nicks* for good measure. If this sounds like the plot of a telenovela, it truly was. Tensions were so thick in the studio that one band member later said you could "cut the atmosphere with a knife, and the knife would start crying."

The Buckingham-Nicks breakup deserves its own rock ballad (in fact, it has several). Lindsey and Stevie had been together since their teens, joined Fleetwood Mac as a package deal, and then promptly fell apart under the pressure of fame. Lindsey, nursing a bruised ego and broken heart, vented by writing "Go Your Own Way," a fiery kiss-off to Stevie that included the immortal line: *"Packing up, shacking up is all you want to do."* That dig insinuated Stevie was sleeping around – a lyric she absolutely despised. "I very much resented him telling the world that 'packing up, shacking up' with different men was all I wanted to do. He knew it wasn't true – it was just an angry thing he said," Stevie recounted, adding that every time she had to sing it on stage, she *"wanted to go over and kill him"*. Yet there they were, night after night, harmonizing on that very chorus. Imagine having to perform a song your ex wrote about what a floozy you are, and smile through it. (Talk about *professionalism* – or masochism.) Stevie retaliated the only way she knew: with her own song "Dreams," a smooth, witchy tune subtly suggesting that Lindsey would regret losing her someday (*"When the rain washes you clean, you'll know"*). It was the gentlest burn possible, but in the context of their situation it was basically Stevie saying, "Bless your heart, you'll miss me."

Across the studio, the McVies were faring no better. Christine McVie decided she was done with John's hard-drinking, "belligerent" behavior – and done with the marriage. She didn't tell him outright, of course. Instead, Christine took up with the band's lighting director, a dashing bloke named Curry Grant, right under John's nose. The kicker? Christine penned the upbeat hit "You Make Loving Fun" about her new affair *and had John play bass on it.* In an act of either mercy or sheer nerve, she told John the song was about her dog just to avoid a brawl. (Imagine being John McVie, laying down a groovy bass line on a love song, thinking it's about your wife's affection for her pup Skipper… only later to learn it was an ode to the guy rigging your stage lights. Irony, thy name is Fleetwood Mac.) To John's credit, he soldiered through the recording like a pro – though one can assume the bottle of scotch was his best friend during that period. In interviews years later, John admitted hearing those lyrics knowing the truth was painful. No kidding: *"I don't have to tell you, but you're the only one"* hits different when you realize you definitely were *not* the only one.

Then there's Mick Fleetwood, the tall, unflappable drummer who was supposed to be the neutral backbone of the band. Ha! Mick couldn't resist getting entangled too. As the *Rumours* sessions rolled on, Mick's wife ran off with his best friend, so Mick consoled himself by slipping into an affair with Stevie Nicks. Yes, that Stevie – Lindsey's now-ex. Because clearly this situation wasn't complicated enough, let's add a drummer–singer fling to the mix! By this point, the band's romantic geometry looked like a jigsaw puzzle designed by a drunk cupid. You had exes singing duets, a divorced couple sharing a stage, and two bandmates sneaking off for midnight rendezvous. According to lore, Mick and Stevie's fling nearly broke the band for good – that was one inter-band dalliance too many. Somehow, they all kept it *just* functional enough to finish the album.

The studio environment during *Rumours* has passed into rock legend. They'd argue violently in the day, not speak to each other except through music, then sing beautiful harmonies by night as if nothing was wrong. One member would storm out of a session, and another would be in tears in the bathroom, and then someone would yell "take five!" and they'd reconvene to nail a take of "The Chain." (Fittingly, "The Chain" is the one song on the album credited to all five members – a Frankenstein's monster pieced together from their jam sessions, with lyrics about loyalty and fate. If ever there was an anthem for dysfunctional unity, that was it.) As journalist Sean Egan wryly noted, Fleetwood Mac's saga was *"a soap opera with the greatest soundtrack of them all."* Fans had no idea in 1977 that when they grooved to "Don't Stop" or slow-danced to "You Make Loving Fun," they were hearing audio alchemy born of pure emotional carnage. The band pretty much bled onto the tape. Lindsey's seething guitar solos? That's him working out his anger at Stevie. Stevie's ethereal vocals on "Dreams"? That's her processing heartbreak. Christine's sunny keyboards? Her attempt to find light while her marriage crumbled. John's bass and Mick's drums provided the heartbeat, steady and true, even as their personal lives skidded off the rails.

Incredibly, instead of collapsing under the weight of all this, Fleetwood Mac soared higher. *Rumours* was not just a hit – it was a juggernaut. 20 million copies sold, Album of the Year, the works. The public sensed the raw honesty in those songs, even if they didn't know the specifics. And Fleetwood Mac, for a while, kept it together *onstage* despite the turmoil *backstage*. Sure, there were fiery moments – like Lindsey and Stevie staring daggers at each other while singing "Go Your Own Way," or Christine pointedly belting "You're the only one" as John stood a few feet away pretending the song was about her dog. Over time, the wounds did heal *somewhat*. They continued making music through the '80s (with new dramas, departures, and reunions – the soap opera never truly ended). Even decades later, the band's reunions would spark old resentments. As late as 2018, Lindsey got ousted from the group amid conflicts with Stevie, proving that this story's final chapter is never fully written.

Fleetwood Mac's romantic battlefield is the ultimate testament to rock 'n' roll chaos: when bandmates marry, divorce, and swap partners, you get legendary music – and legendary emotional scars. It's the classic "dream of the '70s": free love meets stadium tours, and feelings get trampled under the wheels of success. Yet, culturally, there's something awe-inspiring about how they turned private pain into public art. It's almost poetic justice – their breakups yielded a collection of songs the world will sing along to for generations. Call it group therapy with royalty checks. Fleetwood Mac showed that *sometimes the only difference between a toxic love affair and a great album is a recording contract.* As the band themselves sang, *"Thunder only happens when it's raining"* – and boy, did it pour for them. So, what grand lesson can we pry from the wreckage of these rock 'n' roll romances? Gather 'round, because our final chapter has a thesis: the brighter the flame of stardom, the more scorching the burn of a breakup.

Marriage Lesson: The Higher the Chart, the Harder the Fall

By now the pattern is clear: in the music world, the higher the chart, the harder the fall. Our trip through the loves and losses of rock 'n' roll's elite – from Elvis & Priscilla's fairy tale turned cautionary tale, to Sonny & Cher's televised marriage dissolution, to Fleetwood Mac's Shakespearean band drama – illustrates a deliciously ironic truth. When pop idols and rock gods pledge *"till death do us part,"* it often means *"till platinum do us part."* The very forces that launch these couples into superstardom tend to gnaw away at their bonds. It's like a cosmic joke: you can have global adoration or lasting romance, but usually not both.

Consider the next generation of music royalty for further proof. Even Elvis's own daughter, Lisa Marie Presley, couldn't escape the curse. She married the King of Pop, Michael Jackson, in 1994 – a union of two dynasties that made the world collectively gasp, *"What? Those two?!"* It was a bizarre, short-lived spectacle that played out in front of cameras. Who can forget their awkward kiss at the MTV Video Music Awards, with Michael proclaiming, *"And just think, nobody thought this would last."* He was right – it didn't. Eighteen months later, they were done. The higher the profile, the harder the crash. Or recall ABBA, the Swedish pop quartet who epitomized marital harmony on stage while quietly weathering *two* divorces off stage. Björn and Agnetha of ABBA split in 1979, and a year later so did Benny and Frida. These breakups birthed bittersweet tunes like

"*The Winner Takes It All,*" a song so on-the-nose about their situation it hurts – Agnetha sang her broken heart out while the world tapped its feet. *The winner takes it all, the loser standing small…* In the game of love vs. fame, even ABBA – those purveyors of upbeat pop joy – couldn't have it both ways. The bigger their success (they were on top of the world in the late '70s), the more emotionally mangled they became.

The hits keep coming (the songs and the breakups). Whitney Houston and Bobby Brown – a powerhouse diva and an R&B bad boy – thought their union could conquer the charts and their personal demons. Instead, it descended into turmoil and reality TV infamy. Kurt Cobain and Courtney Love were the king and queen of '90s alt-rock, but their marriage was a chaotic cocktail of drugs and drama that ended in tragedy. Ike and Tina Turner – a duo famed for electrifying performances – had a marriage so tumultuous it became a byword for abuse and survival; Tina had to literally fight her way to freedom, and her post-divorce anthem "What's Love Got to Do With It" said it all. And let's not even start on the whirlwind that was Pamela Anderson and Tommy Lee (okay, she's not a musician, but he is): their beach wedding after four days of knowing each other, the infamous stolen tape, the volatility – it's a rock soap for the ages, proving the rule that rockstar romances often self-destruct in spectacular fashion.

Why do these couplings so often combust? Perhaps it's the high-octane mix of fame, ego, money, and temptation. The music industry elevates individuals to near-mythic status – "Elvis the Pelvis," "Cher the Goddess," "Stevie the White-Winged Dove." When two meteors collide, expect explosions. Add gruelling schedules, press intrusion, fan adoration (or jealousy), and often a hearty dose of sex, drugs and rock 'n' roll, and you have a recipe for relationship chaos. Normal couples argue about who takes out the trash; rockstar couples argue when one's face is on *too many* magazine covers or when infidelity rumors make headlines. As one sardonic observer put it, *marriage is hard enough without a tour bus parked on the lawn and a legion of groupies in the guest house.*

Another lesson: these stars often pour their heartbreak into their art, giving the world unforgettable music. We, the public, end up unintentionally *rooting for the drama* because the art that comes out of it is so darn good. Fleetwood Mac's *Rumours*, Sonny and Cher's poignant post-split duet, Adele's entire discography – wait, scratch that, Adele's not in this chapter (though she could be an honorary member of the "higher the chart, harder the fall" club for how many Grammys heartbreak has earned her). The point is, rock 'n' roll romances are almost designed to burn brightly and briefly. They make for great stories and even better Behind the Music episodes. A happy, stable marriage in music-land? Frankly, it's a little boring – it doesn't sell magazines or inspire gossip. But a messy breakup? That's the stuff of legend and box sets.

There are, of course, exceptions that prove the rule. Some musical couples have gone the distance quietly (hello, *Ozzy and Sharon Osbourne*, still snarling at each other after all these years, chaos be damned; or *Johnny Cash and June Carter*, who found salvation in each other). But the very fact that these are notable exceptions underscores how common the splits are. For every love that endures, there are dozens that flame out. It seems the Marriage Gods have a wicked sense of humor when rock stars are involved – perhaps laughing as they toss extra temptation and tribulation their way. It's almost a rite of passage: you get your first #1 hit, you get married at the peak of your fame, tabloids dub you a power couple… and then the Icarus effect kicks in. The fall from grace – or at least from the honeymoon – is swift and public.

So, what's the takeaway from our tour of jukebox couplings? Certainly not that love is doomed – even in rock 'n' roll, hope springs eternal (just listen to any love ballad). But there's a clear *lesson in hubris*: When you live life amplified to 11, expect some feedback squeal. Or to put it more plainly, the rock 'n' roll lifestyle and stable matrimony go together about as well as a guitar and a sledgehammer. The higher they climb the charts – the more adulation, the more pressure – the more likely that love will tumble down the stairway to heaven. Yet, for all the drama and heartache, we can't look away. These stories are hilarious, tragic, and instructive all at once. They remind us that behind the platinum records and glitter, the stars are just as human as the rest of us – only their mistakes are broadcast in Dolby surround sound.

In a witty, roundabout way, maybe that's the true cultural significance of these rock romances. They're the modern myths; our Greek tragedies set to a 4/4 beat. The gods on Mount Olympus (or in Hollywood Hills) struggle with the same follies of love and pride. We watch, we gasp, we sing along to the fallout. And perhaps we even learn a thing or two about our own relationships (Note to self: probably don't marry someone who writes a song called "Go Your Own Way" about you). In the end, the music outlasts the romance. The breakup might be hard, but the songs – the songs are forever. Elvis and Priscilla, Sonny and Cher, the warring members of Fleetwood Mac – their loves crashed and burned, but their legacies remain enshrined in pop culture, equal parts cautionary tale and juicy entertainment.

So the next time you hear a classic love song on the radio, remember the saga behind it. Laugh at the irony, appreciate the artistry born from adversity, and maybe raise a glass to the star-crossed lovers who gave us these stories. Rock 'n' roll romances might not often have happy endings, but they do come with killer soundtracks and a wink from history. In the grand theater of music and love, the final lesson is this: *the spotlight of fame is a hell of a heat lamp for marriage – those who can't stand the heat, end up back on the street.* And as the curtain falls on our chapter, we can't help but smirk at the drama and hum along, because in rock 'n' roll, the wreckage has a rhythm all its own.

Chapter 7

Modern Mania: Brangelina, Kimye & Reality TV Weddings

Modern love has never been more public, more chaotic, or more meme-worthy. In the age of Instagram filters and 24/7 celebrity news, marriage has sometimes turned into a spectator sport. We've seen unions that double as social media events, divorces that dominate headlines, and romances that feel scripted for reality TV (sometimes literally). In this chapter, we dive into three epic marital sagas of our times – the Hollywood spy-thriller-turned-courtroom drama of Brangelina, the high-fashion soap opera of Kimye, and the blink-and-you-missed-it reality TV spectacle of Kim Kardashian's 72-day matrimonial sprint. In the end, we'll wrap up with a tongue-in-cheek lesson for the modern romantics: if your vows are trending, so might your split. Grab the popcorn (and maybe a prenup) – it's going to be a wild ride.

Brangelina: Mr. & Mrs. Smith Go to Court

When Brad Pitt and Angelina Jolie met on the set of *Mr. & Mrs. Smith* in 2004, it was chemistry you could bottle (and plenty tried – tabloids practically exploded). In that 2005 action rom-com, they played a married couple who are secretly assassins hired to kill each other. Spoiler: by the end, they team up and live happily ever after – after blowing up half their house. For a while, life imitated art. The co-stars-turned-lovers became "Brangelina," the ultimate Hollywood power duo. They had the looks, the fame, the sex appeal – and eventually a brood of six children to form a mini–United Nations. Their 2014 wedding was a private, low-key affair (by celebrity standards), but by then they were already de facto married in the public's eyes. They graced red carpets and charity galas, adopted kids from around the globe, and even co-starred in a high-brow art film about a troubled marriage (*By the Sea*, 2015) – talk about foreshadowing. For a decade, Brangelina were *the* couple that "defined the culture," as one magazine put it, idolized as much for their humanitarian work as for their movies.

But if *Mr. & Mrs. Smith* was the sexy meet-cute, the finale was more courtroom drama than rom-com. In 2016, the Brangelina fantasy cracked – no, shattered – with a single headline: Angelina files for divorce. The trigger? Reports swirled about a private jet flight gone terribly wrong – an alleged altercation so bad it sparked an FBI investigation (no, that's not a movie plot, it really happened). Mr. Smith had apparently gone *full* Smith. Within days, Jolie cited "irreconcilable differences" (Hollywood legalese for "this mission has self-destructed") and requested physical custody of the kids. The world was stunned. How could the glamorous do-gooder duo – who once seemed capable of saving orphans by day and starring in blockbusters by night – fall apart in such spectacular fashion?

What followed was a divorce saga so convoluted it made *War of the Roses* look tame. *Conscious uncoupling?* Not a chance – this was an all-out battle. "Since then, it's been anything but conscious uncoupling," Entertainment Tonight quipped about the ensuing legal war. Indeed, the split quickly morphed into a multi-front conflict: a bitter custody fight over their six children, asset squabbles over a \$60 million French château and winery, and dueling PR campaigns that splashed dirty laundry across headlines. One dispute involved Jolie selling her share of their beloved Château Miraval winery (apparently without looping Brad in on the deal), prompting Pitt to sue her in a fit of vintage *he-didn't-approve-the-merlot* rage. She countersued; he countersued the countersuit – it was the kind of legal ping-pong that could put *Law & Order* writers to shame.

Irony had a field day. This was the couple who fell in love playing married assassins, now assassinating each other's character in court. In *Mr. & Mrs. Smith*, Brad and Angelina's characters kept secret arsenals in the house; in real life, they kept secret recordings for custody hearings. In the film, they battled each other with guns and witty one-liners; in the divorce, they battled via lawyers and leaked documents. (At one point Jolie alleged Pitt got physical with one of the kids on that infamous plane ride, painting him as an out-of-control drunk – allegations he vehemently denied. The FBI and child services ultimately filed no charges, but the damage was done.) It's as if *Mr. & Mrs. Smith 2: Courtroom Edition* was unfolding before our eyes, without the Hollywood ending.

Public fascination with Brangelina only grew during the implosion. This was the same voyeuristic thrill we get watching a high-speed car chase on live TV – we can't look away. As one cultural commentator noted, the appeal of *Mr. & Mrs. Smith* was the voyeuristic charge of seeing two glamorous stars play house and then blow it up, indulging our desire to believe even these idols have problems "just like us". Well, wish granted – their real-life marriage turned out to be *far* from perfect. For years, gossip mags had pedestalized Brad and Angie as the beautiful do-gooders who could do no wrong (cue those People magazine covers of "Happy Home!" and "Baby Joy!"). Now, suddenly, they were tabloid fodder of a darker sort: allegations of drinking and screaming fights, children traumatized, heated emails about parenting schedules. Schadenfreude much? Millions followed every twist – from *Team Jolie* vs. *Team Pitt* debates to the internet collectively asking "How's Jennifer Aniston feeling about all this?" (Answer: unbothered, baking cookies with her million-dollar *Friends* residuals, thank you very much).

Perhaps the biggest twist of all is how long the breakup lasted. Brad and Angelina were married for only two years, but spent roughly *eight years* legally untangling that union. (They were together for over a decade, but didn't tie the knot until 2014 – and were done by 2016, at least romantically. The divorce, however, dragged on and on… and on.) To put that in perspective, eight years is four times the length of their actual marriage – a fact the Los Angeles Times dryly noted in its coverage. It's as if they couldn't stop collaborating, even if now the project was "How to Spend Most of a Decade Getting Divorced." Lawyers must have been salivating. By 2019, a judge declared them legally single (so they could, in theory, date other people – and Pitt did, prompting all of us to awkwardly relearn how to spell *Neri Oxman* for a few months). But the custody and financial fights raged for years after. It was only in 2024 – a good *eight years* after Jolie filed – that reports emerged of a final settlement and a collective sigh of relief from Angelina, who was said to be "exhausted but relieved" to finally close the chapter. In Hollywood terms, their divorce was an epic saga, one of the "longest and most contentious splits in Hollywood history". Who needs a marriage that long when your divorce can set records?

Through it all, the *pop culture irony* was rich. This was the duo that once sold us the image of domestic bliss – remember that infamous 60-page W Magazine spread in 2005, where they posed as a 1960s couple with a brood of kids in an idyllic suburban setting? (The shoot was literally titled "Domestic Bliss." You can't make this up.) It was fantasy fulfillment for fans: the glamorous stars playing house, winking at the rumors of their budding affair. A decade and a half later, "Domestic Bliss" had turned into public *dysfunction*. Perfect life a complete fiction? Check. The *Mr. & Mrs. Smith* tagline of two extraordinary people pretending to be normal spouses turned out to have a darker real-life echo: even these extraordinary people couldn't make their own marriage work. As one snarky Twitter user observed, maybe the only thing Brad and Angie *couldn't* save was their own union.

In the end, the Brangelina saga had everything: passion, betrayal, glamour, scandal – a modern myth unraveled. Mr. and Mrs. Smith went to court, and the whole world watched. It's a tale of our times that even the most idolized relationships can self-combust under pressure (and perhaps that *too* is oddly reassuring to us mere mortals). At least we'll always have *Mr. & Mrs. Smith* – two hours of beautiful people blowing stuff up, unfettered by child custody evaluators or winery assets. Ah, simpler times.

Kimye: Fashion, Fame, and Fallout

If Brangelina were the Hollywood demigods of the 2000s, Kimye were the emperor and empress of the 2010s pop culture kingdom. Kim Kardashian and Kanye West's marriage wasn't just a union of two ultra-famous people – it was the collision of two cultural juggernauts, a fashion-fueled, social-media-optimized, cashmere-coated spectacle. Love them or hate them (and plenty of people did both), for a while you couldn't escape them. As Vogue's Anna Wintour herself explained when she put the then-engaged Kim and Kanye on that April 2014 *Vogue* cover – him in a tux, arms around her in a bridal gown – they "define the culture at any given moment" and influence "the way we see it". In other words: Kimye *were* the zeitgeist. And they damn well knew it.

Let's rewind to the origin story. They'd been friends for years before coupling up – Kanye, the outspoken rap genius with a penchant for leather pants and self-comparisons to deities; Kim, the reality TV star-turned-mogul who managed to leverage selfies and savvy into an empire. When they finally got together in 2012, it was like two brands merging. By 2014 they were exchanging vows in a lavish Florence wedding at a Renaissance fortress (because a regular church just isn't epic enough, obviously). The wedding featured a wall of flowers taller than an elephant, Andrea Bocelli serenading Kim down the aisle, and countless camera crews capturing Kim's third trip to the altar (yes, third time's the charm). Their wedding photo – kissing in front of that flower wall – reportedly set an Instagram record for likes at the time. That's Kimye for you: breaking the internet as a side hustle.

Kimye's reign as a couple was marked by high fashion and higher drama. They were fixtures at the Met Gala, turning heads in outfits that sparked a thousand memes (who can forget Kim's 2013 floral sofa dress when she was pregnant with North, or Kanye's blue contacts and bedazzled jacket phase?). They tag-teamed on a *Vogue* cover, sat front row at Paris Fashion Week, and made *his-and-hers* matching style a thing. (One year they even wore matching faux-bleached hair – commitment!) Kanye launched his Yeezy fashion line with Kim as his muse, and Kim's wardrobe evolved from L.A. glam to edgy haute couture under his influence. In the media, they were nothing short of royalty: he called her "my queen," she called him "the most talented" and "creative" person alive. Fame squared, influence cubed.

Yet, behind the gloss and the *couple goals* hashtags, the cracks were always visible if you looked closely. Kanye's larger-than-life personality increasingly stole the spotlight – and not always in a good way. He had a habit of going on Twitter tirades that ranged from hilarious to deeply concerning. One week he'd be proclaiming himself (literally) a god or announcing a run for President (2020 did *happen*, remember?), and the next he'd be feuding with fellow celebs or ranting about, well, anything. Kim often played the role of the supportive partner doing damage control. She stood by during his controversial moments – the Taylor Swift VMAs interruption was pre-Kimye, but there would be others: Kanye's public embrace of polarizing politics, his outspoken comments that sparked backlash (slavery "sounds like a choice," anyone?), and his very public struggles with mental health which sometimes unfolded in real time on social media.

By 2020, the spectacle started to overshadow the love story. Kim, ever the image-manager, was reportedly *exhausted.* In early 2021, after nearly seven years of marriage and four children together, she filed for divorce. Pop culture fans braced themselves – if Kimye couldn't make it, what hope do the rest of us have? But in truth, it wasn't a sudden break. "It's so different from the person that I married," Kim said later, reflecting on how much Kanye had changed. According to her, she couldn't "foresee" the circumstances that led to their split – essentially,

Kanye's transformation into someone she could no longer live with. It's a relatable sentiment (who hasn't watched a partner change in ways you didn't expect?), though most of us don't have to deal with our partner tweeting our intimate family matters to 30 million followers.

The fallout of Kimye's split was as high-profile as the marriage. Kanye, never known for his quiet restraint, made the divorce downright operatic. He aired grievances in song lyrics and on Instagram, sometimes alarmingly so. Case in point: in 2022 he released a music video for the song "Eazy" featuring a claymation figure unmistakably resembling Kim's then-boyfriend, comedian Pete Davidson, whom the video depicts being kidnapped and buried alive. (Subtlety, thy name is not Ye.) The video caused an uproar – was it art, or a threat, or just Kanye being Kanye? Pete Davidson reportedly found the ridiculousness "hysterical," but it was clear Ye was not taking the breakup well. He also took to posting (and deleting) a flurry of accusatory, often incoherent Instagram messages about Kim, about Pete ("Skete," as Ye mockingly nicknamed him), and about how he wasn't being allowed to see his kids as he wished. It was messy and at times uncomfortable – even diehard fans were like, "Dude, maybe log off and chill." Kim, for her part, largely kept a dignified silence in public, breaking it only to plead for compassion for Kanye's mental health at one point, and to gently correct misinformation (like reminding everyone that actually, she was the main caregiver and no, Kanye couldn't just drop by unannounced). When their drama trended, it was literally *world news*. The spectacle of a disintegrating marriage had never been more visible.

Yet amid the chaos, the *business* of Kimye had to be untangled. And by late 2022, untangle it they did – relatively swiftly by Brangelina standards. The divorce was finalized with what appeared to be a fairly straightforward settlement (thanks in part to a solid prenup). The terms? Joint custody of the kids, no spousal support (Kim and Kanye are each worth hundreds of millions, they'll be fine), and Kanye agreeing to pay a whopping $200,000 per month in child support. Yes, you read that right – two hundred *grand* a month. That's about $50k per kid, presumably to keep them in the private schools and custom Balenciaga jackets they're accustomed to. Chump change for Ye when his Adidas Yeezy deal was booming, but after his later controversies and business fallout, one imagines he might be wincing at the bill. Either way, the saga was legally over. Culturally, though, its legacy lives on.

Kimye's story is a cautionary tale of modern celebrity matrimony. On one hand, they were the embodiment of a power couple – they combined their strengths and dominated fashion, music, and media. They truly were, for a time, pop culture royalty: Kim with her reality TV crown, Kanye with his musical accolades and self-styled genius. They even gave us new frontiers in baby naming (North West, Saint, Chicago, and Psalm say hi – move over, Apple Martin). On the other hand, their marriage showed the strain that level of fame and ego can put on two people. Their lives were an open book (or rather, an endless series of Instagram stories). They thrived on attention – until that attention also fueled their undoing. When things got bad, there was no retreating to privacy; it was all out there, a public play-by-play of a power couple's dissolution.

Through it all, Kim remained surprisingly relatable (no small feat given her life). She cried on TV about her marriage ending, she joked on *SNL* that Kanye was "the richest Black man in America, a talented legit genius who gave me four incredible kids – so when I divorced him, you *know* it came down to just one thing: his personality." Ouch, and yet, fair. Kanye, meanwhile, doubled down on being Ye – even as the divorce was being finalized, he was bouncing through a string of controversies and even a quickie new "marriage" (to an employee of his brand) that may or may not be legally legit. In typical Ye fashion, he also announced another run for president. Kim carried on, expanding her businesses (SKIMS is now a billion-dollar brand), studying law, and continuing her reality TV dominion. Life, and brand Kardashian, march on.

In hindsight, the rise and fall of Kimye says a lot about fame in our era. They were a couple built for the spotlight, who rose because of it – and ultimately, fell apart under it. Their impact on fashion and media was undeniable: They made streetwear and high couture collide; they turned mundane marriage moments (like a proposal in a baseball stadium Jumbotron) into viral content; they were *always* trending. And they proved that even the grandest of romances, when conducted as a global spectacle, comes with a cost. The bigger the spotlight, the bigger the shadow. Kimye's marriage gave us some incredible pop culture moments and a soundtrack of hit songs (Kanye's albums from that era, from *Yeezus* to *The Life of Pablo*, often referenced his marriage and family). It also gave us, ultimately, a high-profile split that had everyone from armchair psychologists to legal analysts weighing in.

Somewhere in Calabasas, perhaps, Kris Jenner is still nodding sagely that any publicity is good publicity. But even she would probably agree: it's been one *wild* ride from "Bound 2" (remember that music video of Kanye on a motorcycle with a naked Kim? Classic) to binding legal documents. Kimye had it all, until they didn't. And if there's a silver lining, it's that both seem to be finding their footing individually now – Kim channeling her energy into work and kids, Kanye… working on himself (we hope). The chapter of Kimye in the annals of celebrity history will be remembered for its unprecedented visibility and influence. It was fun, it was outrageous, it was fashion-forward and backward (Crocs with heels, anyone?). And like so many intense things, it burned bright and burnt out. In the end, Kimye taught us that even a match made in pop culture heaven has to live in the real world – and the real world, unlike Instagram, doesn't always come with a filter.

72-Day Spectacles: Kris, We Barely Knew Ye

Before there was Kimye, there was that other Kim K. matrimony – the one so short-lived that by the time your wedding gifts shipped, the marriage was already on the rocks. Yes, we're talking about Kim Kardashian's infamous 72-day marriage to NBA player Kris Humphries. Seventy. Two. Days. That's how long the *marital bliss* lasted between the reality TV superstar and the basketball big man. "Kris, we barely knew ye" indeed – by the time we learned to spell Humphries, he was gone.

Let's set the scene: It's August 2011. Kim is fresh off a whirlwind romance with Kris H., a likeable but somewhat naïve New Jersey Nets player who got swept into the Kardashian vortex. They decide to marry after about six months of dating. Naturally, it's all captured on camera for *Keeping Up with the Kardashians* – and not just the show, but a special spin-off: *Kim's Fairytale Wedding*. This wasn't just any wedding, it was a two-part, four-hour television event on E! Network (because why have a private ceremony when you can share your love with millions of viewers and a few corporate sponsors?). The wedding was a lavish spectacle even by celebrity standards – estimated to cost around $6 million, with 450 guests, three designer wedding dresses for the bride, a multi-tiered cake tall enough to require its own zip code, and enough flowers to make Versailles blush. The couple said "I do" in a Montecito estate dripping with crystals and grandeur. Kim was in her princess moment, and America was invited to watch in high definition. In the TV special, Kim gushed that it felt like "heaven" and Kris (the groom, not the momager, though she was surely gushing too) said it was "perfect".

Then… reality (the actual kind, not the TV genre) set in. The newlyweds went on a short honeymoon to Italy – cut short because Kim had to get back to filming the next season of her show. (Red flag number one: when you literally can't take a full honeymoon because *the show must go on*). Within weeks, cracks started to show. By September, merely a month after the wedding, tabloids were whispering that the couple was already spending time apart. On the show, we saw awkward moments – like Kim balking at the idea of moving to Minnesota for Kris's career, and Kris wondering why there were cameras in his face 24/7 (bless his heart). By late October, just *72 days* into the marriage, Kim Kardashian filed for divorce citing "irreconcilable differences". Translation: this fairytale turned out to be a bedtime story – and not the kind that ends in happily ever after.

The news hit the media like a ton of bricks frosted with fondant. Fans and critics alike were stunned by the sheer brevity of the union. *Seventy-two days?* People joked that Kim's marriage lasted shorter than an NFL season, shorter than a semester at college, shorter than the lifespan of the fruit fly that crashed her wedding cake. The phrase "72-day marriage" became an instant pop culture punchline. Late-night comedians had a field day ("Kim's marriage was so short, they didn't have time to finish the wedding cake leftovers!"). It didn't help that the divorce filing came on Halloween – cue all the "the marriage was the real trick-or-treat" jokes. To the cynical public, this was peak Kardashian – an allegedly scripted-to-the-gills TV wedding followed by a quick divorce, all looking suspiciously like a ratings grab and cash grab. In fact, reports circulated that between the TV rights, sponsorships, and photo deals, Kim earned a fortune off the wedding – figures as high as $17 million were thrown around in the press, while the couple supposedly spent far less (many expenses were comped or discounted for exposure). Whether those numbers are true or exaggerated, the optics were terrible. It appeared as though Kim cashed in on a fake love story, and many viewers felt duped for investing their emotions in the televised nuptials.

Kim vehemently denied it was a sham. "I married for love," she insisted, and not for TV. In a candid blog post after the split, she confessed, "I got caught up with the hoopla," and felt like she was on "a fast roller coaster" that she "couldn't get off". In other words, the show took on a life of its own – and she didn't know how to exit gracefully once doubts set in. She admitted that maybe she *should* have called it off before walking down the aisle, but at the time she didn't want to "disappoint a lot of people". It was a rare glimpse of vulnerability and perhaps the most authentic explanation: the pressure of the spectacle essentially guilted her into going through with a wedding her heart wasn't fully in. (A cynic might add: the pressure of a multi-million-dollar TV deal, but let's take her at her word that emotional pressure was a big factor.)

And what of the other player in this saga, Kris Humphries? The poor guy was reportedly blindsided. When Kim filed for divorce, he released a statement saying he was "devastated" and willing "to do whatever it takes to make it work". That tugged at some heartstrings – he genuinely seemed to have believed in the fairytale. But he didn't stand a chance against the Kardashian narrative machine. He quickly went from being an innocuous doofus on the show to being painted (in some corners of the media) as a clueless, mildly villainous figure who just "didn't get" Kim's life. There were also reports he felt exploited by the whole reality TV apparatus. Humphries even sought an annulment on the grounds of fraud, implying Kim never intended to stay married and just wed him for publicity. The legal battle over that (divorce vs. annulment) stretched on for over a year and a half – in fact, the divorce wasn't finalized until April 2013. (Delicious irony: the legal marriage outlasted the actual coexistence by a huge margin. It took about 18 months to legally dissolve a union that lasted 2 and a half months. Lawyers: 1, True Love: 0.)

The whole affair was a spectacle that highlighted the increasingly blurry line between love and entertainment in the reality TV era. Here was a wedding that garnered 10.5 million TV viewers for the ceremony special – basically a blockbuster by cable standards – only to have the marriage collapse faster than a Jenga tower. It definitely made people ask: Were we all just suckers for watching? Did Kim

Kardashian stage a wedding for ratings? Even *Kris Jenner*, matriarch and manager extraordinaire, later quipped to her daughter in a teasing way, "Longer than 72 days!" when discussing Kim's prospects for a future marriage. When your own mother is roasting you for the short stint, you know it's ingrained in pop culture. The fact that this happened in 2011 and in 2025 Kris Jenner is *still* making tongue-in-cheek comments about it on their Hulu show tells you the staying power of that 72-day punchline.

On a more serious note, the Kim-and-Kris debacle did spark conversation about how reality TV framing can put absurd pressure on personal decisions. The entire lead-up to the wedding was documented and hyped. E! billed it as "Kim's Fairytale Wedding" – and fairytale it was, in the Brothers Grimm sense where things get dark quickly. Kim later expressed regret about rushing and about televising the whole darn thing. In the reunion episode of *Keeping Up* a decade later, she even said she owes Kris Humphries an apology for how she handled things. Humphries himself largely shied away from the spotlight after the divorce, clearly not eager to prolong his 15 minutes of fame earned in that circus.

From a pop culture perspective, however, *we* gained something: a textbook case of reality TV's influence on real-life choices. The 72-day marriage became a yardstick for fleeting celeb marriages (measured in Kardashian Units: 1 KU = 72 days). Whenever another star has a quickie marriage, someone inevitably jokes, "well, at least it lasted longer than Kim's." It's a bit mean, sure, but that's the price of being the poster child for blink-and-miss-it matrimony. And let's be honest, there's a twisted relief in it for the rest of us – your cousin's ill-advised Vegas wedding that got annulled in a week? Not even on the radar compared to the Kim K standard.

The Kardashian spin machine, of course, moved on. Kim's brand was not significantly dented – if anything, the notoriety may have even boosted her fame (there really is no such thing as bad press in Kardashian-land). Within a year, she was dating Kanye West, and the whole narrative shifted to *that* extravagant saga (see previous section!). The 72-day marriage became just a footnote in the larger Kardashian saga, a funny story to be referenced in monologues and interviews. Reality TV, on the other hand, took note: from then on, every *Bachelor* proposal, every *Housewives* wedding, carries the unspoken question – is this love, or is this a plotline?

In conclusion, "Kris, we barely knew ye" encapsulates the absurdity of turning one's love life into a season finale event. It's modern love as content, marriage as a mega-event, and divorce as, essentially, an epilogue that has to be tied up before the next season starts filming. And while it's easy to mock (and boy, have we), there's also a human story in there of a young woman who felt the weight of her own brand and audience so heavily that she went through with a marriage she wasn't sure about. That's the dark side of the spotlight: when your personal relationships become public expectations. If nothing else, the 72-day saga gave us all a handy piece of life advice – maybe don't televise your wedding, and if you do, at least stay married longer than the reruns.

Marriage Lesson: If Your Vows Are Trending, So Might Your Split

After touring the wreckage of these high-profile unions, one can't help but notice a theme: the bigger (and more public) the wedding, the harder the fall. What does it say about modern relationships when we're keeping score of marriage lengths like it's a sports statistic? We live in an era where proposals are flash mobs, weddings are hashtagged extravaganzas, and Instagram feeds turn couples into mini-celebrities in their own circles. Love has become a performance art – and not everyone survives the third act. So, let's step back and glean some satirical words of wisdom from these tales of modern matrimony gone awry.

First off, social media is a double-edged sword in romance. Sure, it's fun to share the cute selfies and gushy anniversary posts – but when you start curating your love life for public consumption, be careful. One study found that couples who post excessively about their relationship tend to actually be less happy than those who post rarely or not at all. (Translation: That friend who writes a 300-word Facebook ode to their spouse every week? Maybe protesting too much.) Constantly projecting "#Blessed #Soulmates #BestHusbandEver" might come across as confidence, but it can also be a sign of insecurity or overcompensation. Meanwhile, the truly content couples are too busy enjoying each other to meticulously document every date night. It's the classic iceberg effect – what you see on the surface (social media) often hides what's underneath (and sometimes that's a Titanic waiting to happen).

With that in mind, here's some witty advice for those seeking Insta-love or otherwise caught up in the spectacle of modern romance:

- Don't treat your wedding like a Hollywood premiere. It's a marriage, not a movie release. If you find yourself spending more time picking a hashtag and filtering photos than talking about life goals with your partner, take a pause. (Your marriage is supposed to last a lifetime; your wedding hashtag will be forgotten by next Tuesday. Priorities!)

- If you need a drone to film your proposal, you might also need a therapist on standby. Grand gestures are romantic, sure. But remember, after the skywriting and fireworks, you two still have to sit in a room together and have, you know, actual conversations. Don't let the theatrics substitute for genuine connection.

- Resist the urge to "Keep Up with the Kardashians" (or the Joneses) when it comes to love. Just because Kim K. had a parade of flower walls and TV cameras at her wedding doesn't mean you need to livestream yours on TikTok. The more you turn your relationship into a public show, the more pressure you create to live up to an image – and that image can become a prison. Sometimes the most #authentic thing you can do is *not* share.

- Remember that a trending hashtag is not a solid foundation. By all means, celebrate your love publicly if you want, but don't confuse online validation with actual viability. 10,000 strangers liking your cute couple pic doesn't equate to one honest, tough conversation about finances or future plans. One is easy, the other is real. Do the real stuff.

- Be wary of the "viral vortex." That's when your relationship milestones become content. It can start innocently: a proposal video that goes viral, a wedding dance that trends on YouTube. Fun! But then you might feel compelled to keep feeding the beast – the perfect pregnancy reveal, the picture-perfect family Christmas card… Until, uh oh, the image cracks. And when it does, the same people who cheered you on might revel in the gossip of your split. Don't let the crowd dictate your relationship's pace or worth.

At its core, the satirical lesson from Brangelina, Kimye, and the 72-Day Wonder is that marriage is not a reality show (or a music video, or a blockbuster film). It's a complex, sometimes messy, often unglamorous journey – and that's okay! When you add the distortion of fame or social media frenzy, it's like trying to read fine print in a funhouse mirror. The image gets warped. Brad and Angelina were playing *pretend normal* in *Mr. & Mrs. Smith* and perhaps in life, until they weren't. Kim and Kanye crafted a spectacle of love that couldn't withstand real pressures. Kim and Kris H. got swept up in a televised fairy tale that crashed as soon as reality reared its head.

The tongue-in-cheek takeaway for the rest of us is not "don't get married" or "don't post your cute couple photo" – it's keep perspective. Go ahead and enjoy the romance, even the spotlight if it shines your way, but remember what's real and what's for show. And if you find yourself composing an Instagram caption about how your spouse is your *sun, moon, and stars* while secretly seething that they left the toilet seat up again – maybe address the latter in private and cool it with the former in public.

In an age where every person with a smartphone is essentially a mini-celebrity broadcasting their "personal brand," it's easy to fall into the trap of turning your love life into performative art. But as we've seen, when a relationship becomes too much of a performance, it can buckle under the weight of its own script. Social media applause is fickle – here today, unfollowed tomorrow. Real love, by contrast, is often quiet, patient, and, yes, a bit mundane at times. And that's not a bad thing.

So if your vows happen to go viral, congratulations on the 15 minutes of fame – just don't be surprised if the internet is taking bets on your split down the line. The same spotlight that makes you trend can also highlight your flaws and feed the naysayers (or legal eagles) when things go wrong. The modern mania around weddings and celebrity relationships is entertaining, no doubt. But behind the snark and satire lies a genuine plea: cherish the personal over the public. Or as a wise, if cynical, observer might put it: happily ever after works better off-camera.

In closing, remember the immortal wisdom that perhaps should be printed on a scroll at every over-the-top wedding: If you court the public's adoration at the altar, you may also face their judgment in the divorce court. In other words, if your vows are trending, so might your split – and in the battle of love vs. the limelight, the limelight usually wins. Keep it real, keep it a little private, and maybe, just maybe, you'll have a shot at a love story that doesn't end as tomorrow's juicy headline. Cheers to that, and may your #forever actually last forever (or at least longer than 72 days).

Chapter 8

VIP Vows: Power Couples & Political Passion

Bill & Hillary: Campaigns and Complications

Bill and Hillary Clinton's marriage has been the stuff of political legend, tabloid fodder, and late-night comedy for decades. They're the original American power couple who turned partnership into an art form (and occasionally a contact sport). The story begins at Yale Law School in the 1970s: two ambitious nerds locking eyes in a library, presumably over a pile of thick law books. It wasn't exactly a Hollywood meet-cute, but sparks flew between the Arkansas charmer in bell-bottoms and the brilliant Illinois girl with thick glasses. Fast forward a few years, and they formed a union where campaign strategy discussions double as pillow talk, and "buy one, get one free" became more than a supermarket slogan – it was essentially Bill's pitch to voters about their political tag-team.

From the outset, the Clintons made it clear: elect one Clinton, and you kind of get the other in the package. Bill Clinton openly touted Hillary as his not-so-secret weapon, joking that supporting him meant two public servants for the price of one. And he wasn't wrong. Back in Arkansas when Bill was governor, Hillary was an active force – a lawyer, policy advocate, and definitely not content playing the quietly smiling spouse in the background. In Washington, she shattered the traditional First Lady mold with the force of a thrown lamp (allegedly one of the Oval Office flying objects during their stormier days). Hillary was put in charge of a health care reform initiative in 1993, a bold move that had D.C. wags dubbing her "President Hillary" only half-jokingly. Pop culture even picked up on the vibe – the Clintons were sometimes compared to a real-life Frank and Claire Underwood (minus, one hopes, the homicidal tendencies). In the House of Cards of real Washington power, the Clintons showed you could be partners in marriage and co-conspirators in policy, finishing each other's sentences and occasionally each other's Cabinet appointments.

Of course, no discussion of Bill and Hillary's partnership is complete without *the* scandal that nearly capsized it: the Monica Lewinsky affair. In the late 1990s, the world learned way more about presidential preferences (cigars, anyone?) than it ever wanted to. It was the ultimate test of the Clinton bond, played out on every magazine cover and newscast. The President famously wagged his finger and declared, "I did not have sexual relations with that woman," and for a moment Hillary appeared on national TV defending him, blaming a "vast right-wing conspiracy" for the rumors. Talk about stand by your man – Hillary did it on live television with gritted teeth and a gaze that could burn a hole through Mount Rushmore. Their marriage became late-night joke material, the *definition* of "complicated." Cynics quipped that the Clintons' was a marriage of political convenience – a power-sharing agreement in which Hillary tolerated Bill's wanderlust in exchange for a shot at the Senate, or even the presidency herself. A Los Angeles Times piece from January 1998 captured an oddly tender moment of the pair slow-dancing on a

Caribbean beach in their bathing suits, a candid photo that turned into PR gold. Bill later admitted he loved that picture (surprise, surprise – it humanized them at a critical time) even though he hadn't realized anyone was snapping photos. Leave it to the Clintons to accidentally stumble into a great publicity moment: even their private romantic dance became a strategic asset.

Hillary's choice to stay with Bill post-Lewinsky became a national Rorschach test. Some saw a savvy political calculus; others saw genuine forgiveness (with a dash of "I'll get my turn later, buddy" determination). She was mocked on SNL, praised on talk shows, and endlessly psychoanalyzed. Yet, through it all, the Clinton partnership endured like a long-running TV drama with shocking twists but unbreakable leads. Indeed, one famous jokey anecdote from the '90s sums up their dynamic: The two are driving through Arkansas when they stop at a gas station. The attendant, as it turns out, is an old boyfriend of Hillary's. Bill, ever the rascal, supposedly teases, "If you'd married him, you'd be the wife of a gas station attendant." Quick as lightning, Hillary quips, "If I'd married him, *he'd* be President." *Ba-dum tss!* Whether that exchange actually happened or is just D.C. folklore, it perfectly illustrates the Clintons' image: Hillary isn't riding Bill's coattails; she's effectively co-driving the whole darn bus.

The 2000s saw the roles start to shift. After Bill left office (amid a frenzy of last-minute pardons and a few pranks – like removing the "W" keys from White House keyboards to troll the incoming George W. Bush staff), it was Hillary's turn to shine. With Bill playing First Laddie in waiting, she became Senator Clinton of New York. Picture this: Bill, the natural extrovert who loves a crowd, had to sit on the sidelines while Hillary glad-handed voters and gave speeches. By many accounts, he was *itching* to jump in, and occasionally he did, sometimes a bit too forcefully. (During her 2008 presidential run, Bill's off-script remarks earned him the role of "campaign complication" more than once.) Still, they campaigned as a duo whenever possible – the wonky power couple in matching pantsuits (okay, only Hillary wore the pantsuits, but Bill's ties often coordinated). Their complexity even seeped into pop culture satire: The Simpsons had episodes lampooning Bill's scandals, and Hillary's steely ambition became a character trope on shows like Parks and Recreation (anyone remember Leslie Knope's reverence for HRC?).

Through health scares, political defeats, and grandparenthood, Bill and Hillary have stuck together. They are *experts* at reinvention and resilience. One minute they're dancing (fully clothed) at an inaugural ball, the next they're on "60 Minutes" doing damage control and projecting unity. They've been married for over 40 years, and in the public eye for almost as long – that's a lot of time to perfect the art of the power couple pose. Yes, the pose: standing side by side, fingers interlocked, both gazing outward toward a shared bright future (or at least toward the cluster of TV cameras). The Clintons have it down pat. Say what you will about their marriage – loving partnership or shrewd alliance (or a bit of both) – it has survived the kind of trials that would send mere mortals to divorce court or a deserted island. Campaigns and complications go hand in hand for these two, but they long ago made a vow *stronger* than oak: not "till death do us part," but "till ambition do us part." And neither shows any sign of giving up ambition anytime soon.

Barack & Michelle: Love in the Oval

If the Clintons are a drama, the Obamas are a certified romantic comedy – the kind that leaves you smiling and believing true love can conquer even the *West Wing*. Barack and Michelle Obama burst onto the national scene and immediately turned the stodgy old First Couple archetype on its head. Here were two people who *genuinely* seemed to like each other, not just tolerate each other for photo ops. They laughed together, hugged in public, shared secret glances, and fist-bumped (scandalous! a First Fist Bump!) on live TV. America hadn't seen anything quite like it. The Obamas were young (by presidential standards), stylish, and very much in love, and they didn't hide it. It was as if a modern Cosby Show-esque vibe had strolled into 1600 Pennsylvania Avenue (minus any problematic off-screen baggage). Barack and Michelle were not just partners in power; they were best friends who happened to run the country on the side.

Their backstory only adds to the legend. They met in the late '80s at a Chicago law firm when Michelle Robinson was assigned as mentor to a summer associate named Barack Obama. Yes, she was literally his boss (at least for that summer). The tall, skinny guy with the funny name had to beg the confident young lawyer for a date – she initially said no (because who wants to date the intern, right?). But Barack was persistent and charming; he wooed her with ice cream and casual strolls, and before long they were an item. If this were a movie, we'd cue the montage of them falling in love over books by Toni Morrison and Stevie Wonder songs. Fast forward to 1992: they got married, Michelle famously teased that Barack's large ears struck her at first ("He's cute, but I don't know about those ears…" she joked later). They came from humble backgrounds – student loans, used cars, the whole relatable young couple package. Little did they know they were headed for the ultimate glow-up: from a starter condo in Chicago to the White House.

Once they hit Washington, the Obamas became *bona fide* pop culture icons. They graced magazine covers like *Vogue* and *Essence*, became fodder for skits (remember Fred Armisen and Maya Rudolph as the Obamas on SNL?), and even inspired relationship goals hashtags. Michelle was dubbed "Mom-in-Chief" and fashion icon, rocking everything from Target cardigans to stunning designer gowns with equal ease. Barack, meanwhile, was the cool dad president, known for dropping mixtapes of his favorite songs each summer and casually singing Al Green's "Let's Stay Together" at a fundraiser (sending hearts aflutter). Their public displays of affection were frequent and genuine – a quick kiss at a basketball game "Kiss Cam," an affectionate shoulder squeeze during speeches, or that famous campaign trail fist bump in 2008 that one pundit ridiculously called a "terrorist fist jab" (the pundit later ate crow for that one). The Obamas basically brought romance to the Oval Office, and the world ate it up like a bowl of Michelle's organic White House garden salad.

But let's not sugarcoat it – maintaining a marriage under the spotlight of global scrutiny isn't a carefree walk in a rose garden (even if that garden is tended by the National Park Service). Michelle has been refreshingly frank that, despite appearances, their marriage is not pure Disney fairy tale. She's joked about times when she *couldn't stand* Barack (imagine giving your husband serious side-eye at a state dinner – she's hinted it happened). In fact, Michelle recently raised eyebrows with a humorous comment that for about 10 of their 30+ years together, she "couldn't stand" him – a reminder that even the

Obamas have their rough patches. As she put it, *"we're just a couple of human beings doing the best we can"*, a revelation that might shock those millions who placed them on a pedestal as the ideal marriage. They've "made a lot of mistakes, ... gotten it wrong", Michelle admits, but they keep "working at it" and it "gets better and better" over time. Imagine that: even the coolest couple on Earth has to work at marriage. Frankly, that admission was a relief to all of us whose idea of a hot date is arguing over Netflix choices. If Barack and Michelle have to compromise and persevere, there's hope for the rest of us!

Throughout eight years in the White House, the Obamas managed to avoid any personal scandals – a minor miracle in modern politics. The biggest controversies were things like Barack wearing a tan suit (cue faux outrage) or Michelle baring her toned arms in a sleeveless dress (cue *gasp* from pearl-clutchers). In other words, nothing remotely salacious. In the absence of real drama, the media often settled for writing about their *love*. Whole articles gushed over the way Barack looked at Michelle adoringly during his inauguration, or how she straightened his tie lovingly before a debate. They slow danced at inaugural balls to Etta James' "At Last," literally having *their moment* while millions watched on TV and sighed. They even gave us tear-jerker moments: who didn't get a little misty when Barack, in his farewell address, thanked Michelle as his best friend and the "nation's new favorite daughter" Sasha and Malia's mom, saying she made the White House a place "that belongs to everybody"? He basically publicly serenaded his wife with praise, and a thousand Hollywood rom-com scripts were instantly put to shame.

The Obamas also mastered the modern art of blending politics with pop culture. Barack went on late-night talk shows to "slow-jam the news" with Jimmy Fallon; Michelle did carpool karaoke and danced with Ellen DeGeneres. They showed up at Hamilton on Broadway like regular fans (sending the audience into a frenzy). They shared playlists and reading lists, as if to say, "See, we're normal people! We just happen to have nuclear codes and a Secret Service detail." Perhaps one of the most delightful pop culture crossovers was seeing Barack and Michelle rocking out in the front row at a Beyoncé and JAY-Z concert, looking like *the coolest mom and dad in the arena.* Yes, the Obamas are part of the Beyhive! That image alone was like a millennial pink cherry on top of their cultural sundae.

To sum it up, "Love in the Oval" wasn't just a cheesy tabloid headline for the Obamas – it was their reality. They demonstrated that a strong marriage can survive and thrive amid the pressure cooker of the presidency. No Oval Office affairs or clandestine soap operas here; just a lot of love, mutual respect, and inside jokes (we can only imagine the ribbing Michelle gave Barack about his struggle to quit smoking or his infamously dad-style jeans). In an era of cynicism, the Obamas gave us genuine relationship goals. They left the White House still holding hands, ready to conquer the next chapter together – producing Netflix shows, writing memoirs, and continuing their reign as one of the world's most admired couples. It's enough to make you believe that sometimes, the nice guys (and gals) really do finish first – and they do it arm-in-arm with their soulmate, even as they wave goodbye from Marine One.

Beyoncé & JAY-Z: Music, Money, Matrimony

When it comes to the entertainment world, Beyoncé Knowles-Carter and Shawn "JAY-Z" Carter are the alpha and omega of power couples. They're basically American royalty – think King and Queen of Pop Culture, with a combined net worth higher than some country's GDP and a fanbase (the Beyhive + whatever Jay's super-fans are called) that treats them as near-deities. But even deities have their drama. In the case of Bey and Jay, their marriage has been a mix of chart-topping collaborations, meticulous brand-building, *and* the occasional elevator scuffle that launches a thousand memes. It's *music, money, matrimony*, with a heavy dose of PR magic holding it all together.

Their saga began in the early 2000s like an R&B meets hip-hop fairy tale. Beyoncé was a rising star fresh out of Destiny's Child, and Jay-Z was the suave mogul-rapper with a Midas touch. They teamed up professionally before they ever admitted anything personally – dropping hits like "'03 Bonnie & Clyde" and the mega-smash "Crazy in Love" in 2003. The chemistry in those songs and music videos was off the charts; fans weren't *just* crazy in love with the track, they were convinced these two beautiful people *must* be in love with each other. They were right. Bey and Jay were dating on the sly, but unlike the oversharing celebs of today, they kept their relationship fiercely private. No red carpet canoodling, no confirmation to press. In fact, for years they played coy about their status, which only made the public more intrigued. It was the will-they-won't-they of the music world, except everyone kind of knew *they did, they definitely did.* When they finally tied the knot in a super-secret ceremony on April 4, 2008, it was so under wraps that gossip rags were left scrounging for leaked photos of Beyoncé's ring and Jay-Z's satisfied grin.

As a married duo, the Carters carefully cultivated an image of glamorous mystery. They weren't doing joint sit-down interviews about their home life – oh no. Instead, they gave us glimpses through lyrics and onstage moments. They became the masters of *show, don't tell.* Need to announce a pregnancy? Beyoncé will just drop her mic, pop open her sequined blazer and rub her belly at the MTV VMAs, leaving the crowd (and poor clueless Jay in the audience) stunned and ecstatic. Want to respond to a nasty rumor? JAY-Z might address it in a rap verse, or Beyoncé will throw a pointed lyric into a song that her fans dissect like it's the Da Vinci Code. This tight control served them well as their brand (and family) grew. They had a daughter, Blue Ivy, in 2012, and the world all but melted down at how adorable this mini-Beyoncé was. (Never mind that her parents promptly trademarked her name – branding is everything, folks). By the time twins Rumi and Sir arrived in 2017, the Carters' image as a loving, powerful family was firmly in place – glossy Instagram announcements and all.

But even the mightiest of couples hit turbulence. For Bey and Jay, the storm came in the form of infidelity – Jay-Z's, to be specific – and Beyoncé's wrathful, artful response. Enter the now-legendary chapter of their marriage: Lemonade. In 2016, Beyoncé released *Lemonade,* an album (and accompanying film) that took the world on a rollercoaster through her psyche. It was raw, poetic, visually stunning, and *very clearly* narrating a story of a woman scorned and reborn. Lyrics about cheating and betrayal ("He only want me when I'm not there / He better call Becky with the good hair") sparked a global spectator sport of Who-Did-What-To-Beyoncé. The Beyhive detectives went into overdrive hunting for the mysterious "Becky," while talk shows and think pieces debated Jay-Z's apparent fall from grace as the once-perfect husband. The album ended with themes of forgiveness and reconciliation, but the message was clear: Queen Bey was hurt, and she wasn't staying silent. Instead of a press conference or a tell-all interview, she turned her pain into a platinum album and HBO special, forcing the world to feel *every ounce* of her Texas fury and her ultimate grace in choosing to heal. As one analysis put it, *"'Lemonade' wasn't just an album; it was a personal reckoning"* – Beyoncé using art as therapy and public catharsis.

JAY-Z didn't remain silent either – but true to their style, he responded through music as well. In 2017, he released *4:44*, essentially a mea culpa set to a beat. On the title track, he apologizes for "womanizing," and throughout the album he reflects on the pain he caused, even addressing how his actions could have cost him his family. In an interview, Jay admitted, *"The hardest thing is seeing pain on someone's face that you caused... We were using our art almost like a therapy session."*. Marriage counseling by way of songwriting – leave it to the Carters to pioneer that approach. By openly processing their marital struggles through music, they managed to turn a tabloid crisis into a triumphant narrative of growth. It's as if they said, "Fine, world, you want to gawp at our drama? We'll give you front row seats – but you're gonna pay $15.99 for the album on Tidal first."

And pay we did. *Lemonade* was a smash, *4:44* was critically acclaimed, and together Beyoncé and Jay-Z emerged from the storm seemingly stronger. They went on a joint tour in 2018 pointedly titled "On The Run II" – basically presenting themselves as an unbreakable Bonnie-and-Clyde team on the run from negativity. During that tour, on a massive screen, they even displayed renewed wedding vows and home video of their kids, as if to say, *we're good now, y'all*. The public ate it up, and the Carters' empire kept expanding. Business ventures, endorsements, Ivy Park athleisure wear, champagne brands – you name it, they built it. Through it all, they maintained tight control of their image. These two could teach a masterclass in PR (in fact, their longtime publicist Yvette Noel-Schure probably *could* teach that class). They perfected the art of the carefully crafted statement. Remember the notorious elevator incident of 2014? (How could anyone forget? That grainy leaked video of Beyoncé's sister, Solange, going full ninja on Jay-Z in an elevator while Bey stands by looking elegantly unbothered is burned in our brains forever). The gossip mills went wild with speculation – what did Jay do to provoke *that*? In response, the family released a measured joint statement acknowledging the incident, denying the juiciest rumors, and delivering the gem: "At the end of the day, families have problems and we're no different. We love each other and above all we are family.". In one swoop, they both normalized their squabble *and* basically told everyone to mind their own business. It was a PR spin worthy of an Olympic gold medal.

Pop culture has immortalized the Carters in myriad ways. They've been name-dropped in countless songs (sometimes by themselves – Jay-Z rapping "She was the queen, I was her soldier" about Bey, for instance). Beyoncé's alter ego "Sasha Fierce" and Jay-Z's moniker "Hova" (as in Jehovah, a God of rap) feed into a mythology where their marriage is like a celestial event. They even took over the Louvre in Paris for a music video ("APES**T"), casually posing in front of the Mona Lisa – a power move if there ever was one, basically saying "we're a masterpiece too." There's a sly humor in their domination: the Carters know the world is watching and they wink at us through art. Example: Jay-Z once joked in a lyric, *"You know you made it when the fact your marriage made it is worth millions / Lemonade is a popular drink and it still is.".* He was referencing how their very marriage's survival became a pop culture moment as big as their music. It's meta, it's cheeky, and it's true.

Now, more than two decades since their first date (reportedly at a sushi restaurant – humble beginnings for a couple now worth over a billion), Beyoncé and Jay-Z stand as a testament to modern marriage's possibilities. They're partners in every sense: lovers, co-parents, co-creators, and co-CEOs of Brand Carter. They've shown that matrimony in the spotlight can be both profitable and provocative. Sure, rumors still swirl on occasion (the Beyhive will forever be ready to sting "Becky with the good hair" if she ever shows up), but by and large the Carters have reclaimed their narrative. In their world, when life hands you lemons, you make Lemonade – and then you win Grammys for it, sell out stadiums, and maybe launch a champagne line called "Ace of Spades" to toast to your resilience. 🎉

Marriage Lesson: Behind Every Powerful Partnership Is a Great Publicist

What do our three superstar couples – the Clintons, the Obamas, and the Carters – have in common besides joint bank accounts large enough to fund NASA? They know the importance of image. Love, trust, and mutual respect are crucial, sure. But when you're a power couple, so is the ability to curate your story for the public. In the cynical, media-saturated age we live in, perhaps the tongue-in-cheek truth is this: *behind every powerful partnership is a great publicist.* In other words, keeping a marriage rock-solid is hard enough; doing it while the world watches requires spin doctors, brand managers, and a flair for theatrics.

Consider how each of these duos handled their challenges. The Clintons practically wrote the book on war-room damage control. In the '90s, during scandal season, they brought in image experts and advisers by the dozen. There were press conferences, televised apologies, photo ops galore. When things got especially dicey, they retreated to Martha's Vineyard or Camp David with Chelsea in tow and re-emerged smiling for the cameras, as if to say, "Nothing to see here, folks – just a normal family enjoying a beach picnic (totally not strategizing about impeachment defense, nope)." They understood that optics can trump reality. If enough people see you looking happy and *presidential* together, they just might keep believing in you. Bill and Hillary's enduring partnership is in no small part due to their shared mastery of this game. They *embraced* the fact that they were a brand – sometimes even cheekily referencing it. (Hillary's 2016 presidential campaign once tweeted on their anniversary, "@BillClinton, let's do this for another 40 years" with a photo of them – a bit of romantic corniness, yes, but also a message of unity for voters).

The Obamas, for their part, didn't face sex scandals or betrayals – but they too were extremely savvy about image. In their case, the image was *authenticity*. Their "great publicist" was the aura of genuineness they projected. They let us see just enough of their private adorableness (those hugs, those goofy smiles, Michelle calling Barack "honey" in public) to make us feel like we knew them, while still maintaining boundaries. They brilliantly balanced highbrow and pop culture: one minute hosting state dinners with five-course meals, the next doing a fun dance to Bruno Mars on the White House lawn. Their White House photographer captured candid moments of them *actually* being affectionate and kind to each other – and those photos went viral as propaganda for true love. Think about it: a picture of Michelle affectionately touching Barack's face at a basketball game became a news story in itself. Was that orchestrated? Perhaps not the emotion, but certainly the *sharing* of it. The Obamas recognized that in the 21st century, a political power couple can strengthen their influence by becoming cultural icons. And so they did – carefully, intentionally, yet seemingly effortlessly.

Then we have Beyoncé and JAY-Z, who operate their marriage like it's a top-secret startup nearing a billion-dollar IPO. No detail too small to control; no narrative too big to bend in their favor. They've navigated the roughest waters by turning turbulence into art (literally monetizing their marital therapy sessions). It's hard to think of a savvier PR move than what Bey and Jay pulled off with Lemonade and 4:44. They managed to say *everything* about the state of their union without ever sitting across from Oprah crying into the couch pillows. Instead, they let the music and visuals do the talking – a high-wire act of personal revelation and *brand reinforcement*. By airing just enough dirty laundry to make a hit album (but not so much that it permanently stains the Versace sheets), they got sympathy, respect, and profit in one fell swoop. And when private footage *did* leak without their control (ah, that elevator… ✦), they responded with polished unity – the statement heard 'round the world about family problems and forgiveness. You can bet a team of publicists burned the midnight oil drafting that one, every word vetted by the Carters themselves to hit the right tone. Result? Crisis contained, brand intact.

So, what's the grand lesson for the rest of us, gleaned from these VIP vows? Aside from "maybe don't marry someone with a wandering eye or a propensity to write diss tracks about you," it's that *every* relationship could use a bit of PR savvy. No, you don't need a personal publicist to follow you and your spouse to Costco, spinning your cart disputes into positive narratives (although imagine the press release: "Smiths seen debating cereal choices, in spirited display of communication and compromise!" 😃). But it wouldn't hurt to take a page from these power couples when it comes to presenting a united front. They remind us that partnership is partly showmanship. It's about being on the same team and letting the world know it. It's handling conflicts behind closed doors and coming out smiling (even if one of you had to sleep on the couch... or in the Clintons' case, maybe the Lincoln Bedroom). It's understanding the value of a well-timed gesture – be it a hand squeeze at a press conference or a surprise duet on stage – to reinforce your bond.

Finally, in true cheeky chapter-concluding fashion, let's bullet-point a quick Power Couple PR Playbook for any aspiring dynamic duos out there:

- Embrace the Brand: Like the Clintons, don't shy from being seen as a package deal. Wear those matching power suits (or at least coordinate your messaging). Unity is your USP – Unique Selling Pair. (Bill's BOGO deal taught us well!)

- Put Love on Display (Selective Display, that is): Channel your inner Obama and let genuine affection shine when it counts. A public fist bump or an inside-joke smile at the right moment can do more for your image than a thousand press releases.

Just maybe skip the full make-out session on live TV – keep it classy, folks.

- Control the Narrative: Master the Beyoncé-Jay method of addressing drama on *your* terms. Got issues? Talk it out in private, then decide how (or if) to share. Maybe it's a joint statement full of grace under pressure. Or heck, drop a surprise album and let the art do the talking. When life gives you lemons… remix them into Lemonade and win a Grammy.
- Never Let 'Em See You Sweat: Present a united front, come hell, high water, or internet gossip. If you have to fight, fight privately (or in a soundproof elevator 😜). In public, you're Bonnie and Clyde, Barack and Michelle on date night, Bey and Jay on the run – ride-or-die, through thick and thin. And if a rogue question catches you off guard, have a practiced smile or a witty deflection ready. In the court of public opinion, confidence and composure are king and queen.
- And Yes, Hire That Great Publicist: Media savvy isn't innate to all of us. Don't be ashamed to take a little professional advice on managing your image. Even the pros do it – you think the Clintons went through the '90s without a horde of consultants? Or that the Carters hit "send" on that statement without PR pros on speed dial? Please. A skilled publicist or at least a well-read friend can help craft your couple narrative, whether it's for a *New York Times* profile or just curating the best shots for your Instagram anniversary post.

In the end, the marriages of Bill & Hillary, Barack & Michelle, and Beyoncé & JAY-Z teach us that love and power are a high-wire act. It takes *dedication, trust,* and a dash of shrewd strategy to stay balanced. Behind the scenes, these couples have undoubtedly shed tears and weathered storms that would send lesser unions scrambling. But front and center, they project strength, style, and solidarity. That's no accident – that's calculated couple genius.

So here's to the power pairs who make it look easy (even when it definitely isn't). May we laugh at their antics, learn from their playbooks, and maybe apply a bit of their savvy to our own humble lives. Because if there's one thing we've gleaned from these VIP vows, it's that happily ever after is equal parts passion and PR. And in the immortal words of Beyoncé (aimed at her beloved hubby after some hard-earned forgiveness): *"Hold up... they don't love you like I love you."*

Chapter 9

Lightning Marriages & Encore I Do's

Kim K & Kris H: A Slam Dunk Disaster

Kim Kardashian's 72-day marriage to NBA player Kris Humphries was a slam dunk – into an empty basket. In 2011, the reality star's lavish nuptials had all the makings of a fairy-tale spectacle: a custom Vera Wang gown, hundreds of guests (including A-list pals like Serena Williams and Eva Longoria), and a televised two-part special grandly titled *Kim's Fairytale Wedding: A Kardashian Event*. The whole affair reportedly cost around $10 million – complete with comped luxury extras, from the invitations to the towering cake – yet thanks to shrewd sponsorship deals (Kris Jenner even scored a pre-wedding facelift in the package), the celebrity bride and groom might have actually profited from their own wedding. That's right: this short-lived union was not just holy matrimony, it was *monetized* matrimony.

For a brief moment, Kim and Kris's over-the-top "I do" was the hottest show in town. More than four million viewers tuned in to watch Kim marry her basketball beau in Montecito, California, with Robin Thicke crooning for their first dance. But behind the photogenic smiles and A-list attendees, cracks showed *early*. The couple were bickering almost up to the altar; at the rehearsal dinner Kim half-joked to a friend, "Is it normal to hate my husband?" – while poor Kris Humphries obliviously chowed down on prime rib in the background. (Pro tip: if the thought *"I kinda hate my fiancé"* crosses your mind during the engagement, that's a *red flag* the size of a Kardashian's diamond ring.)

Seventy-two days. That was the official length of Kim and Kris's wedded "bliss". To put it in perspective, 72 days is shorter than the lifespan of a pet goldfish, and significantly less time than it takes to watch every season of *Keeping Up with the Kardashians*. It's also about how long it takes for a Kardashian to change hair colors. By Halloween 2011 – just *over two months* after the storybook ceremony – Kim filed for divorce, citing "irreconcilable differences". Cue the collective eye-roll of the public, who had barely finished flipping through Kim's $1.5 million exclusive wedding photo album spread when news broke that the marriage had crumbled faster than a week-old wedding cake.

Kris Humphries, bless his 6-foot-9 heart, was reportedly blindsided by the split. He issued a flustered statement about being "devastated" and willing to do whatever it took to make it work. The NBA big man apparently thought this covenant meant overtime, not a sudden knockout in the first quarter. But Kim had already mentally left the arena. What followed was a divorce battle that dragged on far longer than the marriage itself. Kris contested the divorce and even sought an annulment on the grounds of fraud, claiming the whole thing was a PR stunt. (The man had a point – the wedding did get higher ratings than some NBA finals.) He allegedly demanded a multi-million dollar payout to quiet the "fraud" allegations, despite a solid prenup. In the end, after two years, several court dates, and untold awkward reality TV moments, the divorce was finalized in 2013 – officially freeing Kim to move on to her next chapter (spoiler: it involved a future rap mogul and a couple of kids).

Perhaps the most absurd footnote of this lightning-fast marriage was the fate of the engagement ring: the 20-carat diamond stunner that had been proudly flashed on magazine covers was later auctioned off by Kris for a "mere" $749,000 – a steal at roughly one-quarter of its rumored value. If that doesn't scream *depreciation*, what does? In true Kardashian fashion, Kim landed on her feet – and with a new love – not long after. Even her momager Kris Jenner couldn't resist joking about the 72-day fiasco years later, quipping that she hopes Kim's next marriage will last "longer than 72 days". Talk about setting a low bar. Kim K's short-lived slam dunk wedding may have been a dazzling public spectacle, but it goes to show that when you fast-forward romance for the cameras, you might just end up with a very short highlight reel.

Nicolas Cage: Quickie Quirks & Vegas Vows

If impulsive marriages were an Olympic sport, Nicolas Cage would be gunning for the gold. The Oscar winner and living meme has a well-earned reputation for eccentricity – and that extends to his whirlwind love life. Case in point: in March 2019, Cage got hitched in Las Vegas to a makeup artist named Erika Koike, and their wedded bliss lasted all of four days. Yes, four days – roughly the runtime of a long *Lord of the Rings* movie marathon. Cage filed for an annulment so fast it set a Hollywood record, citing that he was too intoxicated to understand what he was doing when he said "I do". (Imagine *Leaving Las Vegas*, but as a comedy: man meets woman, drunkenly marries her at a casino, then snaps to reality before the complimentary champagne goes flat.) Not surprisingly, he also claimed his bride had hid "the full nature of her relationship with another person," which is Vegas-speak for "maybe she had a secret boyfriend on the side". The whole episode was so absurd that even Cage – a man who once outbid Leonardo DiCaprio for a dinosaur skull and owns a pyramid tomb in New Orleans – found it a tad too bizarre.

But the four-day Vegas vow is just one chapter of Nic Cage's quickie quirks. Let's not forget his equally fleeting union with the daughter of the King of Rock 'n' Roll. In August 2002, Cage married Lisa Marie Presley (yes, Elvis's only child) in a lavish Hawaii ceremony. This pairing of Hollywood weirdness and rock 'n' roll royalty seemed intriguing – for all of 107 days, anyway. After roughly three and a half months of marriage, Cage filed for divorce, later admitting that they "shouldn't have been married in the first place". Considering Lisa Marie's own impulsive marital history (she'd famously wed Michael Jackson in another short-lived spectacle), perhaps this match was doomed from the start. Their split was swift and decisive, a high-speed crash of a relationship that left both parties shaking their heads once the dust settled.

Nicolas Cage's journey to the altar (and then rapidly to the courthouse) has more twists than a plot from one of his action movies. His first marriage, to actress Patricia Arquette in 1995, began with a truly outlandish courtship: legend has it that a young Nic was so smitten, he embarked on a scavenger hunt devised by Arquette, hunting down impossible treasures like J.D. Salinger's autograph and a black rose to prove his devotion. (When your romantic quest sounds like a deleted scene from *National Treasure*, you know it's peak Cage.) They married in a private ceremony – only to separate nine months later, proving that even completing a love quest is no guarantee of "happily ever after." Cage's other romances have been equally unpredictable. He's collected wives almost as often as he's changed hairstyles for movie roles: five marriages at last count, ranging from a waitress-turned-wife in a small ceremony to his latest bride, a demure Japanese actress thirty years his junior. Through it all, Cage maintains an earnest, hopeless romantic streak beneath the eccentric exterior. This is a guy who named his son Kal-El (after Superman) – he's never been afraid to profess his love in the grandest terms, and while the declarations don't always pan out, it's whimsical, it's absurd, and it's undeniably entertaining – the man's love life is basically a one-man rom-com where he plays both the swooning hero and the comic relief.

One has to admire Cage's audacity: he dives headfirst into matrimony the way he dives into offbeat film roles – completely committed in the moment, consequences be damned. Whether he's exchanging vows on a whim under the glitzy lights of Vegas or wooing a woman with over-the-top grand gestures, he exemplifies a particular Hollywood breed of impulsive romantic. Sure, most people might think twice (or thrice) before saying "I do" yet again, but Nicolas Cage operates on a different wavelength – one where the motto seems to be *"If at first you don't succeed, marry, marry again."* Quickie marriages and quirky breakups have become as much a part of his legend as stealing the Declaration of Independence on screen. At least we can say this: life with Nic Cage is never boring – even if you might need a seatbelt (and a good lawyer) for the wild ride.

Drew Barrymore: Triple Take Tie-the-Knots

Drew Barrymore has always worn her heart on her sleeve – sometimes with a wedding ring to match. The beloved actress has said "I do" three times, each marriage a testament to her impulsive, hopeful romanticism and her resilient spirit when things (inevitably) went sideways. Unlike the spectacle of Kim K or the eccentric escapades of

Nic Cage, Drew's lightning marriages carry a kind of endearing earnestness – a Hollywood wild child who kept believing in love, no matter how many times it blew up in her face (or ended with divorce papers).

Her first trip down the aisle was practically a Hollywood legend in itself. In 1994, at the tender age of 19, Drew spontaneously married a 31-year-old British bar owner named Jeremy Thomas after a whirlwind six-week courtship. The setting? His Los Angeles pub, in the wee hours of the morning, with a minister friend suggesting *"Hey, why not tie the knot right now?"* as if ordering another round of drinks. Drew later quipped they were doing it "the old-fashioned way. Kind of." Well, "old-fashioned" flew out the window fast: the newlyweds didn't even make it to their three-week anniversary. In fact, they split just 19 days after saying "I do" – roughly the shelf life of milk. Before the ink could dry on the marriage certificate, Drew realized she'd made a *teensy* mistake. She reportedly knew it was wrong *on the very day* of the wedding. She essentially bailed on the relationship during what should have been their honeymoon – legend has it she flew off to Hawaii for a film shoot and phoned her brand-new husband to say "Actually, never mind," leaving him home bewildered. (Ouch.) The divorce was filed promptly, with Drew later alleging that Thomas had used her for money and a green card. She even cheekily referred to him as "the devil" in an interview not long after. Moral of that story: sometimes Prince Charming is really just a frog in a tuxedo, and a spur-of-the-moment barroom wedding at 5 AM might *not* be the recipe for everlasting love.

A few years and a lot of life experience later, Drew took a second chance at vows – this time with someone closer to her world: comedian Tom Green. The two met while filming *Charlie's Angels* in 1999 and quickly became the kind of oddball couple fans adored. In July 2001, they pulled off a surprise wedding in Malibu, with Drew barefoot and beaming and Tom goofily grinning. This marriage lasted a bit longer – a whopping five months or so – before reality (and irreconcilable differences) set in. It turns out surviving a cancer scare and a house fire in the span of a year (yes, those both happened during their brief union) was easier than surviving marriage itself for these free spirits. Tom filed for divorce by that December. Both of them were heartfelt yet frank about the split. "[We] were young and kind of idiots," Drew reflected years later. They loved each other, no doubt, but love alone doesn't magically impart the maturity to make a marriage work – especially when you're two Hollywood kids juggling fame, youth, and, apparently, literal flames. Still, in true Barrymore fashion, she and Tom parted on good terms. In fact, they reunited as friends on her talk show decades later to reminisce fondly about their misadventure, proving that sometimes ex-spouses can evolve into amicable acquaintances once the smoke (from the house fire, and the marriage) clears.

Third time's the charm, right? For a while, it seemed so. In 2012, Drew married art consultant Will Kopelman, and this time she traded impetuous drama for what looked like domestic bliss. She embraced the role of wife and soon, mother – having two daughters whom she dotes on. For four years, Drew appeared to have found the stable, *normal* family life she craved after a childhood of Hollywood chaos. But even this fairy tale had an expiration date. By 2016, Drew and Will announced their split, ending what was by far her longest marriage. There was no explosive scandal, just a realization that their storybook wasn't headed for a happily ever after. Drew described their divorce as "the death of a dream" – a poignant phrase that encapsulates how painful the end of that chapter was for her. She had finally done things in a grounded, grown-up way – courtship, kids, the quiet domestic life – and still wound up with a broken heart. The two co-parent amicably and remain on friendly terms. After three trips to the altar and three emotional exits, Drew has become a bit more cautious about legally binding love. She's outright vowed *never* to get married again – "Never, never, never, never," she said emphatically in 2020. And who could blame her? As she joked, after three divorces you realize you might not be "good at this" and you don't exactly crave a fourth try.

Yet, here's why we can't help but adore Ms. Barrymore: she hasn't soured on *love* itself one bit. "I will never get married again," she clarified, but it doesn't mean she's closed off her heart. She's open to romance, companionship, and all those swoony feelings – she's just not rushing to sign any marriage certificates. In a way, Drew's love life has been like one of her romantic comedies in fast-forward: a series of meet-cutes, grand gestures, quirky mishaps, and heartfelt monologues, all playing out in real time. And through it all, she remains, somehow, optimistic. After each heartbreak, she bounces back, dusts herself off with a disarming grin, and keeps going, an enduring symbol of hopeful romantic resilience. If lightning marriages are mistakes, at least she's the type to learn and grow – and laugh – from them.

Marriage Lesson: Just Because You Can Doesn't Mean You Should

What's the takeaway from this cavalcade of lightning marriages and repeat "I do's"? For one: just because you *can* get married on a whim in Vegas (or live on TV, or in a bar at 2 AM) doesn't mean you should. Impulsive matrimony is a bit like bungee jumping – exhilarating in the moment, but you better hope that cord (of commitment) is strong, because the fall can be rough. In the cases of Kim, Nic, Drew, and countless other stars who've tried the quickie wedding approach, it seems many were more in love with *the idea of love* – the romance, the attention, the dramatic gesture – than prepared for the actual work of marriage. It's easy to get swept up in a whirlwind courtship and think, "Sure, let's get married, what could go wrong?" (Answer: a lot, very quickly.)

The difference between being in love and being in love with *love* itself is subtle but crucial. Being in love means you see the other person, warts and all, and still sign up for the long haul. Being in love with love means you're basically casting yourself in a rom-com, complete with elaborate proposal and Cinderella wedding, without checking if your co-star is truly compatible long-term. Kim Kardashian, by her own later admission, was caught up in the wedding fever and fairytale fantasy – the camera-ready romance – and perhaps didn't truly know or even particularly like Kris Humphries all that much when she walked down the aisle. Nicolas Cage has chased that giddy rush of passion to the altar so many times you'd think it was a hobby; he falls hard and fast, like a movie hero, but real-life love isn't always wrapped up in a neat two-hour runtime. Drew Barrymore's nuptial adventures show us the eternal optimist who kept leaping, arms open, hoping each time *this* would be the lasting love – only to learn that love is not a straight-up Disney movie, and even adorable free spirits have to come down to earth eventually.

So, just because you can hire an Elvis impersonator on a whim and get hitched under neon lights, or throw a multi-million dollar televised wedding extravaganza, doesn't mean it's your happily ever after. The chapel might be cheap, but divorce lawyers are expensive – especially when the whole world is watching. Our trio of lightning brides and grooms each learned in their own ways that the real marriage begins when the vows end, and that's the part you can't fast-forward through. Impulsive marriages make for great headlines and humorous anecdotes (with enough distance and hindsight), but they also leave real scars and lessons learned the hard way.

In the end, the hopeful note is that all these folks grew from the chaos. Kim Kardashian moved on to build a family (and an empire) with someone else, seemingly wiser from the 72-day debacle. Nicolas Cage, eternal romantic, is apparently happily married *again* as of this writing – proving that even after epic flameouts, he won't quit chasing that lasting connection (fifth time's the charm?). Drew Barrymore turned her heartbreak into humor and personal growth, focusing on her kids and career and learning she doesn't need a ring on her finger to validate her happiness. The lesson for us ordinary folks? Love is wonderful, but rushing into marriage is like trying to microwave a gourmet meal – you'll get something hot and fast, but the middle might be cold and half-baked. Take your time, keep your perspective, and remember that saying "I do" is easy, but doing what it takes to make it last is the real challenge. And if all else fails and you do end up in a lightning marriage of your own... well, at least you'll have a hell of a story to laugh about later.

Chapter 10

Happily (Not) Ever After:
Lessons from the Aisle

From Nile to Netflix: A Love Story Timeline

Once upon a time, long before dating apps and Instagram proposals, love stories were literally the stuff of legend. Take Cleopatra and Mark Antony – a power couple for the ages, with enough drama to rival an entire season of a Netflix soap. Picture it: Cleopatra, the Egyptian queen, making her grand entrance on a golden barge down the Nile, dressed to slay (quite literally) as the goddess Aphrodite. She arranged the ultimate meet-cute with Roman general Mark Antony by sailing in with purple sails, silver oars, and servants fanning her with exotic perfumes. It was as if she said, "Why swipe right when you can stage an entrance so extra that your future boyfriend's army forgets they're in a war?" The spectacle worked – Mark Antony was captivated by Cleopatra's over-the-top charm, and the two embarked on a passionate alliance that made headlines in ancient scrolls. Their romance had it all: political intrigue, lavish parties, battles, and an ending so dramatic it inspired Shakespeare – complete with a double suicide by sword and snake (talk about commitment).

Fast-forward a couple millennia, and dramatic duos are still hogging the spotlight – just with different costumes and platforms. For a modern contrast, consider a 21st-century pairing like Priyanka Chopra and Nick Jonas, who crafted a love story that spanned continents and hashtags. She's Bollywood royalty; he's a pop music prodigy. When these two collided, the result was a multicultural romance fit for the streaming era. Sure, Nick didn't conquer empires for Priyanka, but he did something almost as brave: slid into her DMs and shut down an entire Tiffany's store to buy a ring. Their courtship was a whirlwind – a brief public dating period before he popped the question – and then came the wedding(s). Oh, the wedding! Cleopatra had the Nile, but Priyanka and Nick had a multi-day extravaganza in Rajasthan so opulent it made a royal wedding look like a quick courthouse elopement. There were fireworks, multiple outfit changes, and a guest list that felt like the Met Gala meets a UN summit. The festivities were meticulously documented on Instagram, with every outfit and even the vodka brand tagged for posterity. People buzzed about their ten-year age gap – but if Cleopatra could woo both Julius Caesar and a younger Mark Antony, what's a decade difference? Their union became a global spectacle, proving that the more things change, the more love stories still feel like epic productions.

And let's not forget the saga of Sophie Turner and Joe Jonas, a couple that gave us a thoroughly modern twist on matrimonial theater. She was Queen in the North on *Game of Thrones*; he was a pop culture prince in a boy band. Their romance might not have shaken empires, but it did momentarily break the internet – especially the night they spontaneously got hitched in Las Vegas. No golden barge for Sophie; instead, she and Joe opted for a neon-lit chapel with an Elvis impersonator officiating and Ring Pop candy in lieu of diamond rings. They even had a DJ live-streaming the ceremony (because if Diplo doesn't Instagram Live your wedding, did it really happen?). In a scene that could have been a Netflix rom-com if it weren't real, the bride rocked a chic white pantsuit and the vibe screamed "Vegas rock 'n' roll elopement." Yet, despite the fun-loving start, even Sophie and Joe's chapter had plot twists the bards of old would appreciate. By the time tabloid whispers emerged of trouble in paradise, fans were clutching their pearls (and Ring Pops), realizing that fairytales in Hollywood might dissolve faster than candy on the tongue. From Cleopatra's grand finale to a Jonas fairytale turned cautionary tale, the timeline of love is littered with proof that "happily ever after" often comes with an asterisk. Different eras, different tech, but one constant remains: love has always been a grand performance, and humans never tire of watching the show.

When Passion Meets PR

In the golden age of Hollywood and the wild world of Instagram, one thing has become clear: sometimes a love story isn't just a romance – it's a brand merger. When passion meets PR, the line between a sincere relationship and a calculated publicity stunt is blurrier than a Vaseline-lensed Kardashian selfie. Consider the phenomenon of the celebrity "it-couple" portmanteau. Once upon a mid-2000s time, we had "TomKat" – Tom Cruise and Katie Holmes – a pairing that practically came with its own logo and theme music. The world watched their every move, from Tom's spontaneous couch Olympics on Oprah where he literally jumped for joy declaring his love, to their lavish Italian castle wedding complete with fireworks. It was as if the relationship was co-produced by Paramount Pictures and the

Scientology Network. For a while, TomKat were a Hollywood power duo brand: he was the blockbuster hero, she was the doe-eyed newcomer turned Mrs. Movie Star. They graced magazine covers, ignited gossip columns, and even their baby's arrival (hello, Suri) was front-page news. Of course, passion-powered PR has a dark side: when the love story started cracking, the narrative spun into damage control. By the end, Katie's escape from the marriage was so stealthy and sudden – executed in true thriller fashion – that you'd think it was scripted (and in a way, it was: by divorce lawyers and PR teams).

Then there's "Bennifer," arguably the OG celebrity portmanteau that set the standard for modern media frenzy. We're talking Ben Affleck and Jennifer Lopez, a couple so glittery that tabloids nearly combusted in the early 2000s. They were everywhere – on red carpets and in music videos – a bankable entity whose every Starbucks run was photographed and dissected by the media. They even got engaged with a pink sparkler the size of a small planet. But when your romance turns into a summer blockbuster, there's a risk of public fatigue. By 2003, the media attention on Bennifer's planned wedding was so intense that the couple infamously postponed the ceremony just days before, citing "due to the excessive media attention" that would have spoiled their joy. In plain terms, their love couldn't compete with the paparazzi circus. (Ironically, nearly two decades and several marriages later, Bennifer 2.0 rose from the ashes in the 2020s, proving that sequels happen even in love – and yes, the paparazzi still went wild.)

Modern lovebirds have taken note: if you're a celebrity couple, you're not just merging hearts, you're merging fanbases. Instagram influencers and YouTube vloggers turn relationships into revenue streams, launching joint channels and cute couple hashtags. It's as if every date night needs a sponsor and a professional photographer. Think of today's high-profile pairings: when Kanye West and Kim Kardashian (a.k.a. "Kimye") united, they weren't just a couple; they were a cultural force that could break the internet at will. They literally graced *Vogue* as a package deal, with Kim in a wedding gown on the cover and Kanye at her side – high fashion and reality TV saying "I do." Their marriage was a perfect storm of passion and PR: he got a boost in the fashion world; she got a credibility upgrade in the music/art scene. Together, they spawned trends, kids, and headlines with equal fervor. And yet, with so much image-crafting, sometimes we all wondered: where does the PR end and the passion begin? When Kim and Kanye coordinated their outfits or their outrage, was it love or a savvy media strategy?

It's not just the A-listers – even royals and politicians play the PR love game. Take Prince Harry and Meghan Markle, who spun a transatlantic fairy tale that upended the British monarchy's stodgy media playbook. Their romance had all the fairy-tale tropes (secret dates, whirlwind engagement, fairytale wedding) and then a plot twist – they quit the royal family for Hollywood agents and Netflix deals. Love collided with "The Firm's" PR, and the resulting saga became a multi-season tabloid drama the whole world binge-watched. The lesson? In public life, love is never just between two people; it's a full-blown production. Brands get built – sometimes literally, as power couples launch perfumes, fashion lines, or charity foundations together – and the relationship itself becomes a 24/7 media campaign. The red-carpet PDAs, the joint interviews, the his-and-hers matching power outfits – it's all part of selling the idea of "us." And when cracks show? Well, that's when the official statements get issued ("We have amicably decided to part ways while remaining the best of friends…"), each word manicured by publicists. In the end, passion-meets-PR is a double-edged sword: it can amplify love into legend, but it also turns a breakup into front-page news. When you turn your marriage into a brand, a divorce can feel like a corporate merger falling apart – complete with stakeholders, spin, and a public poised with popcorn waiting to see what happens.

Fame, Fortune, and Final Straws

If love is a battlefield, as Pat Benatar once sang, then celebrity love is a full-on gladiator arena – complete with cheering crowds, sharp objects (looking at you, Twitter), and the occasional career casualty. It's no wonder so many famous unions crash and burn spectacularly. Let's face it: maintaining a blissful relationship is hard enough without a spotlight following your every move. Now toss in colossal egos, hectic schedules, and a social media ecosystem ready to slide into your DMs at the first sign of trouble, and you've got a recipe for romantic combustion.

One common culprit behind famous breakups is the classic ego clash. Imagine two megastars in one household – it's like having two divas fighting for the same mirror. When both people are used to being the center of attention, compromise can turn into a contact sport. Remember the film *A Star Is Born*? Now imagine living it. When two stars both need to shine, their brilliance can blind them to the teamwork love requires.

Then we have the modern menace: the Instagram DM disaster. Back in the day, royals might have worried about intercepted letters or a courtesan whispering in the king's ear. Today's equivalent? A juicy direct message landing in the wrong hands. We've seen high-profile relationships rocked by the dreaded screenshot reveal – the modern equivalent of a letter intercepted by the wrong person. Even squeaky-clean pop stars aren't safe: one minute you're a heartthrob, the next your flirty DMs are viral memes and late-night punchlines. The truth is, when you're famous, temptation is everywhere and privacy is nowhere. A moment of poor judgment – or even an innocent joke misread – can explode a marriage faster than you can say "receipts."

And let's not overlook the seemingly mundane but deadly "scheduling conflicts" – the PR-friendly phrase that glosses over a multitude of marital woes. When stars cite busy schedules as the reason for splitting, it sounds so civilized, as if they just couldn't synchronize their Google Calendars and decided to call the whole thing off. But read between the lines: this often means one person was in New Zealand filming for six months while the other was on a world tour, and the only thing holding their marriage together was a patchy FaceTime connection. Even the strongest bonds can fray when you're literally never in the same time zone. Cleopatra and Mark Antony at least went to battle *together* (well, until Actium…); modern celebrity couples are lucky if they can battle spotty Wi-Fi to have a dinner date over Zoom. The distance dilemma is real – humans aren't great at sustaining romance through phone emojis alone. And when the rare reunion is a red-carpet event with cameras flashing, well, it's hardly intimate quality time.

For every high-profile flameout, there's usually a cocktail of these issues shaking up the drama. Take the meltdown of Kim Kardashian and Kanye West: their marriage survived rap feuds, fashion fiascos, and four kids, but ultimately buckled under the weight of Kanye's very public personal struggles (and perhaps an ego that even Kim's business savvy couldn't rein in). One day they're *Vogue's* couple of the year, and the next she's lawyering up and he's ranting on social media – a case study in how life in the spotlight can amplify the cracks until a whole dam breaks. Or recall Brad Pitt and Angelina Jolie (Brangelina), once the definition of Hollywood glamour and humanitarian partnership. Their breakup had everything: rumors of a blow-up argument on a private jet, custody disputes, an FBI investigation. It was a far cry from their *Mr. & Mrs. Smith* days of sexy capers. The very traits that made them fascinating – two beautiful, ambitious people with a brood of kids and global careers – also made their split a spectacle. When things went south, it wasn't just a family matter; it was international news with more plot twists than a telenovela.

And for a truly eye-popping case of love on the rocks, look no further than the infamous 72-day marriage of Kim Kardashian and Kris Humphries. It had all the buildup of a fairy tale – a televised wedding special, a multi-million dollar ceremony, a dress fit for a princess – and all the staying power of a snapchat. It's as if once the credits rolled on the wedding episode, reality (the non-scripted kind) set in and the whole thing collapsed under its own weight. Before the ink was dry on the $10,000 invitations, the divorce papers were in the mail. If that's not a paradox of our times – turning love into a media extravaganza and then having real life kibosh the fantasy in record time – what is?

So why do these relationships so often go up in flames? Because being married to fame is like a throuple: you, your spouse, and the entire world in your business. Every marriage has "final straw" moments – but for celebrities, those straws are scrutinized, magnified, and often monetized. A fight that a normal couple might resolve in private can become tabloid fodder and Twitter trending gossip, adding pressure that would implode even the steadiest bond. It's telling that many celebrity couples describe their breakups with tidy phrases like "we grew apart" or "we want different things." Underneath those clichés, you can imagine the exhausted sigh of two people who barely saw each other between premieres, who juggled fan expectations and their own ambitions, and just… ran out of steam. In short, staying in love while also staying at the top of your career and in the public eye is a juggling act of chainsaws. And when one drops, it's *messy*.

Marriage Lesson: If History Teaches Us Anything, Love Is Grand—Until It's Tabloid Fodder

After this whirlwind tour through love's hall of fame (and shame), what grand lesson can we take away? Perhaps that love is a splendid thing – until you add an audience. History and pop culture agree on one point: public love stories have a habit of going south with spectacular flair. It's almost as if the universe (or the gossip gods) can't resist a juicy narrative. The moment a couple's private passion becomes a public obsession, the countdown to some kind of downfall begins. Cleopatra and Mark Antony learned this the hard way. Their epic alliance enthralled the ancient world but also made them enemies of Rome, and it literally changed history when it fell apart – their defeat and deaths marked the end of one era and the start of another. Skip to the 21st century, and while a breakup might not topple empires, it can definitely crash websites and sell magazines.

Why do public love stories so often derail? Irony has a role to play. The very elements that make these romances captivating – the glamour, the larger-than-life quality, the sense that it's a story unfolding before our eyes – are what also make them precarious. When everyone is watching, there's pressure for a relationship to be *perfect*, or at least perfectly entertaining. It's like being on a never-ending stage: you can't flub a line or have a bad day without an audience noticing. So when reality inevitably defies the fairy tale (because let's face it, even Cinderella and Prince Charming would eventually bicker over who takes out the trash), the fall from grace is that much more dramatic. A private squabble becomes "trouble in paradise?" headlines. A trial separation becomes a public guessing game. Basically, the peanut gallery becomes a very opinionated third wheel.

Another takeaway from our jaunt through romantic history is that technology may change, but people don't. From gossiping courtiers in Julius Caesar's time to Twitter trolls dissecting the latest celebrity breakup, we humans love to watch love – and we love to watch it unravel. The court of public opinion has been in session for centuries. Henry VIII's marital drama was literally a national crisis (church schism, anyone?) – a tabloid tale of its day albeit with more swords. Fast-forward to modern Hollywood, and we have pop stars and movie idols engaging in their own high-stakes romances and recriminations, just on a digital stage. Remember when Gwyneth Paltrow and Chris Martin announced their split as a "conscious uncoupling"? Even a breakup became a PR-coached performance piece. Different terminology, same spectacle: everyone is trying to control the narrative of love gone wrong.

So, is the lesson to avoid love altogether, or to at least date in obscurity and never ever start a joint TikTok account? Not exactly. Perhaps the real wisdom is to keep some parts of love sacred and off-camera. The happiest couples in Hollywood often are the ones who fly under the radar, prioritizing actual relationship work over photo ops. Ultimately, whether you're a queen of the Nile or a queen of the red carpet, love works best when it's treated as a relationship, not a reality show. When we strip away the spotlights and audience applause, we're left with two people who have to navigate life's ups and downs together. That's hard enough without a box-office opening or world tour in the mix. Love is grand, no doubt – it can inspire empires and ballads and really excellent Instagram content. But as soon as it turns into public property, it tends to become, well, tabloid fodder.

So maybe take a satirical (but sincere) lesson from those who have waltzed down this aisle before us: if you find yourself starring in your very own epic love story, enjoy the grandeur and drama – but perhaps keep the audience at arm's length. That way, when the credits roll on your romance, you have a better shot at "happily ever after," rather than "happily (not) ever after." In the end, the smartest lovers learn from history: love deeply, laugh at the drama – and maybe leave the spotlight to the professionals.

Epilogue

The Final Curtain Call on Celebrity Love

The curtain falls on our tour of Hollywood's most dramatic "I do, I did, I'm done" stories, and what a ride it's been. We've seen lovebirds soaring on cloud nine with paparazzi in tow, then watched the same duos stumble spectacularly off their pedestals. In this book, we laughed (and maybe cringed) at fairytale weddings with $10,000 cakes and diamond-studded gowns, only to witness those marriages unravel faster than a celebrity's Oscar-night hairstyle in the rain. Celebrity marriages truly are the high-wire acts of romance: no safety net, millions watching, and a very public splat at the bottom.

Soaring High, Crashing Hard

Let's take a moment to revisit some of our favorite power couples and their kamikaze love stories. Remember *Brangelina* – the king and queen of Hollywood who proved that even having a dozen kids (okay, six) can't guarantee a happy ending? They went from playing *Mr. & Mrs. Smith* to living Mr. vs. Mrs. Smith. And who could forget *Kimye*? Kim Kardashian and Kanye West were a match made in trending-topic heaven – he, a musical genius with a God complex; she, a reality TV star turned mogul. Together, they broke the internet on the regular. But not even an extravagant Florence wedding, four kids, and a shared love of monochrome outfits could save Kimye from a meltdown worthy of its own Netflix limited series.

Then there's *Bennifer*. Oh, Bennifer – the celebrity portmanteau that launched a thousand gossip columns. Ben Affleck and Jennifer Lopez gave us a rollercoaster in two acts. Act I had all the makings of a Hollywood classic: a *Gigli* box-office bomb and a pink diamond engagement ring the size of a small country. That saga ended just hours before the altar (proving that sometimes love *does* cost a thing – namely, the bill for canceling a lavish wedding). Fast-forward nearly twenty years, and Act II saw Bennifer rising from the ashes like a phoenix. In a plot twist no screenwriter would dare, they finally tied the knot and got the happy ending after all.

And these are just the headliners. We've covered the ones that burned bright and flamed out fast: from quickie Vegas vows that ended before the buffet went cold to legendary serial spouses treating marriage licenses like trading cards. *Elizabeth Taylor* married (and divorced) Richard Burton twice in a double feature for the ages, and Pamela Anderson said "I do" so many times even she might need a spreadsheet to keep track. The pattern is clear: when it comes to celebrity unions, the only thing more over-the-top than the romance is the breakup that follows.

Combustible Chemistry: Why They Can't Have Nice Things

So why do these celebrity marriages combust with such glorious fanfare? Consider this my expert (okay, semi-sarcastic) analysis of the recipe for a high-profile romantic disaster. Take two beautiful, ambitious people, add fame (and a dash of narcissism), shake well, and stand back. In case you want specifics, here are the top reasons our beloved star duos go from "crazy in love" to just plain crazy:

- Too Many Egos, Not Enough Spotlight: When both partners are superstars, it's like having two divas and only one mirror. Sharing is caring – until one career rockets ahead. If one spouse is booking Marvel movies while the other's last project was a straight-to-streaming dud, trouble's brewing. Resentment becomes the real third wheel.

- Schedules Busier Than a TikTok Trend: World tours, film shoots in Bora Bora, 16-hour set days – celebrity calendars laugh at the concept of "date night." Absence might make the heart grow fonder for a while, but six months apart shooting on different continents is basically a built-in trial separation.

- Temptation, a Permanent Plus-One: Let's face it, Hollywood parties make the Garden of Eden look like a daycare. Attractive co-stars, flirty DMs, exes popping up when they see you on a magazine cover – fidelity in Hollywood is about as common as a low-key Kardashian wedding.

- Public Pressure Cooker: Imagine your last breakup, now imagine it unfolding with the whole world watching and weighing in on Twitter and TMZ – one rumor about "trouble in paradise" can become a self-fulfilling prophecy faster than you can say "no comment."

Mix all of the above with the usual marriage challenges we mere mortals face (miscommunication, different priorities, in-laws… or in Hollywood's case, monster-in-laws on reality TV), and you've got a recipe for disaster. It's a miracle any of these couples last beyond the honeymoon Instagram post. The fact that some do feels like a cosmic fluke.

The Last Laugh (and Lesson)

As we close the book – literally – on these tales of matrimonial mayhem, what's the final takeaway? Consider this the ultimate marriage lesson served with a wink: Love is a deluxe, non-refundable rollercoaster ride. Everyone straps in thinking they'll beat the odds – hope springs eternal when you're standing at the altar.

In the end, the grand lesson isn't "don't get married" (where's the fun in that?). It's knowing exactly what you're signing up for. That rule applies as much to Hollywood A-listers as it does to us regular folks, since on your wedding day everyone feels like a superstar. Marriage will test your limits (and, if you're famous, your lawyer's limits). It will magnify your flaws like a 10× zoom lens on an HDTV – every wrinkle, every misstep caught in ultra-high definition. But if you're lucky, it will also bring out your best, in those fleeting moments between the red carpets and Twitter fights.

And if it all goes sideways? Well, you pick yourself up, dab on a little metaphorical concealer, and try again. Maybe even again and again – just ask J.Lo, who collected engagement rings like Pokémon and still found her happily ever after.

Worth the Ride

After all the glitz, gaffes, splits, and makeups, one truth stands out brighter than a giant sparkler on a celebrity wedding cake: love, with all its glitter and wreckage, is still worth the ride. Sure, it might crash and burn, leaving a trail of designer-clad wreckage on the boulevard of broken dreams. But for those sublime moments atop the Ferris wheel – the world at your feet, your paramour by your side – most of us would line up and ride again.

So let's raise a glass to hope and the starry-eyed belief that the next love could be the one that sticks. Go big or go home in love, and keep the faith in love and your sense of humor intact. After all, the show's not over – the next great love story (or spectacular split) might be just around the corner, and you won't want to miss it.

Mic drop.